HOW I DID IT

BUILDING A LAW PRACTICE THAT WORKS FOR YOU

WRITTEN BY: EDUARDO A. MAURA, ESQ.

EDITED BY: LUIS QUESADA, ESQ.

HOW I DID IT: BUILDING A LAW PRACTICE THAT WORKS FOR YOU

FOREWORD

I have known Eduardo for many years, as a friend, colleague, referral source, co-counsel, and respected attorney. He and I both started our law firms around the same time, and with about the same years of experience. I have always been impressed by how closely aligned our values are, and the vision each of us have for the future. He is building a law firm of professional, enthusiastic, and admirable practitioners, who are passionate about getting results. I am honored to consider Eduardo an ally, and look forward to many more years to come.

ERIC P. GROS-DUBOIS, Esq.
Founder, EPGD Business Law

Eduardo has built a successful, client-centered law firm from the ground up. His insights on building and growing a firm are invaluable to any lawyer thinking of hanging up their own shingle.

OSCAR A. GOMEZ, Esq.
Managing Partner, EPGD Business Law

In an industry that lacks authenticity and vulnerability, Eduardo's *How I Did It—Building a Law Practice That Works for You* is a much-needed breath of fresh air. Among lawyers, there is no shortage of those wanting to share their successes and their big victories, but rare are those who let down their guard and let you really see them during the difficult times. In this book, Eduardo pulls back the curtain and gives you a rare glimpse into what it takes to go from immigrant to law firm owner in the US. The hard times, the good times, and everything in between, Eduardo tells it exactly how it is.

In addition to sharing his story from humble beginnings to owner of a successful law firm, in this book, Eduardo also gives insight into how to start a practice that can grow into something to be proud of. In his characteristic genuineness, Eduardo does not claim that his way is the only way, or even the best way, but only that it is the way he did it, in the hopes that you may take something of value from his journey and the lessons he learned along the way.

But this book is much more than a "how-to" book on building or running a practice. Eduardo also gives you a glimpse of what law school was like and how ruthless practicing law in South Florida can be where unethical opponents abound. And as if that wasn't enough, Eduardo brings it full circle by taking you deep behind the scenes of a high-stakes, cross country federal trial with far-reaching, real-life consequences for his clients.

All in all this book is, like its author, an amalgamation of unique life experiences, an incredible story, and thought-provoking material. If you're a lawyer thinking of starting your own practice, or wondering what it takes to make it when you start from scratch, this book is definitely for you.

IGOR HERNANDEZ

Partner, Cornish Hernandez Gonzalez

CONTENTS

INTRODUCTION

Three things motivated me to write this book. First, I love practicing law at my own small firm. I'd probably still love practicing law somewhere else, but I am confident that it would not be nearly as fulfilling. Second, to share my experience of building the firm, the errors I made, the things that worked, and explain to those who may not know it well, the landscape of this industry. Third, to help law students and young lawyers to build their own law firm and to not be afraid to do so. As a non-natural at business, and with limited people skills, I understand first-hand what it is to want to work for yourself—knowing that you can be good at the law part, but not having that collateral non-law related set of skills that will allow you to practice in the environment you wish to practice. This is at the end of the day what a small law firm is: to be able to practice law the way you see it should be practiced and in the environment that you want to practice.

There's an additional, less practical reason why I wrote this. I have this utopian dream in which we live in a world where there's no "big law." Massive corporations do intentional wrongs against consumers or small businesses, and they do not get to use their unlimited resources to pick this massive firm with the top talent in the world to defend their wrong actions and defeat a meritorious consumer claim represented by an average talent limited-in-resources solo practitioner. If there were a million solo or small practices, big law would not exist, they would not have a monopoly on talent, and evil corporations (the evil ones, because there are good ones) would not have the ability to go to this super large firm which, from the start, will have the upper hand on the case. In my utopian legal landscape, the field is, at least a little, more level. If this book makes one lawyer-reader start a small practice, it has achieved its purpose and the field is a tiny more level.

The tips and advice described here are empirical. I have not personally read many books regarding law firm creation, or law firm maintenance. In fact, while there may be a lot of books about law firm management, the literature about law firm creation is rare. Even rarer is the literature about creating a firm in the world of internet, technology, and readily accessed knowledge. But though I have not read a book about "law firm creation," I do read a lot about different topics, including law, business, science, psychology, neuroscience, physics, philosophy, and self-improvement. I even study calculus. And if I can say something preliminarily is that, reading a lot, about different things, has helped me in my law firm. I feel that this overall acquired knowledge informs a lot of my decisions.

The content described here has a specific target: small firms. This content is likely not as applicable for medium or large firms. The Hogan Lovells, Latham & Watkins, Kirkland & Ellis, or Baker McKenzies of the world probably follow other principles, business models, and methods. Further, even within the "small firm" world, this content is less applicable to PI firms, or volume-type practices, those where the stuff to lawyer ratio is greater than 1:1. It is more applicable to firms that develop a niche area (or a few) and that cater to a stable clientele—which is the reality of most small firms.

Finally, the content in this book, while at times technical, is meant to be less of an objective manual on how to create and maintain a law firm, and more the sharing of my own experience doing it. It intends more to answer the "how I did it" question and less the "how is done" question. I want you to know things beyond methods or procedures, but the personal struggles I faced building a firm with no money, no knowledge, no mentor, and little talent. Hopefully, my answer to the "how I did it" question gives you and your firm some tips as to the "how is done" that can help you and you can implement in your own experience.

CHAPTER 1
HOW I DID IT

1.1. What Led Me to It

Before coming to the United States, I was part of a right-wing Catholic religious community. I had devoted eight years of my life to that community as a consecrated lay, which means you cannot marry or have sex. This will be the subject of another book, but long story short, that community had a thing for intellectual life. They valued intellect, knowledge, logical analysis, education, and culture. If you were good intellectually, you could achieve a higher status in that community. Always "status" craving, I tried to seek an intellectual type of path in that community. Though they did not think I was good enough to belong in the intellectual elites of the community, they did let me formally study philosophy and theology, which I loved (you needed consent for this, you could not just study whatever you wanted). Imbued in the humanities from an early age, and decently competent intellectually, I thought law school was a good fit for me.

In mid-2007, I had just lost a small restaurant business that I had bought with the savings from working 100 hours per week for four years, undocumented, doing all sorts of jobs. The experience of losing my restaurant reinforced the "I don't want to be poor" feeling I've always had. I didn't want to have to start again, for the third time now. I thought I should seek something that nobody could take away from me, like a degree or a license. I wanted a career that would make me money. The only two options I saw was doctor or lawyer. I was already 28 or 29. I didn't think medicine was an option because it was too long. Plus, I didn't like it either. But I didn't like the law either. At that point, I liked nothing. Philosophy was probably the only field that I liked intellectually. But I was not going to study philosophy. Philosophy equaled being poor. Money was a big thing for me. I refused to be poor again.

After I lost my business, I got a job at a personal injury law firm. A 38-year-old Peruvian American guy owned the firm. The guy was a bit of a dick. My job consisted of scanning documents all day. My pay was $9.50 dollars an hour. It was literally the most boring job I've ever had. I had to grab a box of files, take the papers off the fasteners, take all the staples out, and run the papers through the scanner. Then, I would walk to my 4x2 desk in a corner of the firm, isolated, go to the scanner digital folder in the computer, and "save as" in the respective file. Once done, back to the scanning machine to do the same, over and over, for 8 or 9 hours. I hated this job. It was so boring that I would read the documents I was scanning to distract myself. (Remember, no Facebook or smart phones to browse). Reading the documents, I thought, this is not rocket science. I also carefully observed the firm owner, who had 70 employees and a lot of money, and I thought the guy was of average intelligence at best. My thinking at that moment was "if this guy can do it, so can I." At the firm, I asked some of the people there how long law school takes and they told me three years after a bachelor's degree. I thought that was great. Time was a concern of mine given my age. I looked into transferring some of the credits I had earned from back home in order to complete a bachelor's degree in the fastest way possible. Working at this boring firm, scanning documents, had pushed me over the edge. I was going to pursue a legal career with all my strength. I didn't care if I didn't like it. I didn't care how I felt. I thought feelings/passion was a dangerous guidepost. Law was a decent, honorable, well-paid profession, so I was going to pursue it no matter what.

At the time, I was dating a Cuban girl who had a job as a secretary in the maintenance department at FIU. I knew that if you worked there, FIU paid half of your tuition. I also thought that working there, it would be very convenient to take classes there as well. I told my girlfriend to find me a job at FIU. Any job. The office next door to her was the key shop. "Key Control" we called it. The department that handles all keys, door repairs, and locking systems on campus. She learned of a position as a "locksmith helper." It paid $12 an hour. I told her to talk to the manager to try to get me an interview. I filled the application online. Eli, the manager, gave me an interview. It was hard to persuade Eli. He thought I didn't want to be in Key Control long term, and I just wanted the job to go to school. He was right. But notwithstanding that, I was able to persuade him that I would do a fantastic job as a "locksmith helper." He gave me the position. This was around early 2007.

Once hired, I worked my ass off. I showed Eli my commitment to the work. Not only did I learn locksmithing superfast, but I would do 15 work orders per day where the rest would do just 5 or 6. In less than 4 weeks, I was already doing locksmith work and, around that time, a locksmith position opened. The position paid $2 more, which was significant at the time, so I enrolled in a locksmith course by mail. The company would mail you your assignments. A padlock you needed to unlock. A lock you needed to re-key. You name it. The program was supposed to last around 3 months, but I did it in five or six weeks. Once I got my certification, Eli gave me the locksmith position; $14 dollars an hour with benefits at a state university. There was also overtime permitted, which allowed me to make decent money.

One of the first things I did as an FIU worker was drive my little golf cart to the admissions office. At the admissions office, I met a nice lady who loved my story—especially the fact I wanted to get an education. She walked me through the process of being admitted in detail, and most importantly, how to transfer my philosophy credits from Peru. Based on my conversations with her, it became clear to me that, no matter what I liked, which was unknown, the fastest path to a bachelor's degree (what I needed to get into law school) was a philosophy degree. So I had a lot of homework to do: bring my official credits from the Peruvian institutions, obtain official translations here in the U.S., obtain an official "validation" of the credits by an accredited entity in the U.S., take the TOEFL exam and score higher than 600 points (of 750 total), and the most important part, take the never easy Law School Admission Test (LSAT), with a score good enough to get into FIU (around 153 plus). Later also, I had to do all the paperwork to apply for financial assistance.

I did all the paperwork validations, and I was able to start classes in the spring semester of 2007. I remember driving my little golf cart to my classroom, taking off my FIU maintenance shirt like Superman, and putting it in the little glove like compartment in the golf cart and going to my class. I couldn't believe it. I was going to classes at a university in the United States. It was incredible to me. Like most dreams, they deflate a bit once you achieve them, but I believe I've always had a good sense of gratitude and appreciated what it meant for me. Undocumented for four years, from Pueblo Libre, taking classes at a U.S. university. It was a BFD, to quote Joe Biden.

The timeline to make it through law school was tight. Here, you need 120 credits to get a bachelor's degree. You need 200 to get the same in Peru. So, though I had not completed a degree in Peru, I had a lot of credits. Especially because the religious community had transferred me to another city in the middle of my studies where I basically had to start over. They don't really care whether you are enrolled in University X in City X or the consequences of a transfer on your career. They just transfer you, and you must go. They say it's God who wants the transfer, so it's hard to argue with that. Long story short, I had more than 120 credits, but they were not all transferable. FIU accepts a maximum of 60 credits; 90 with a special exemption, which I was able to obtain. Technically, I needed only 30 credits to complete a bachelor's degree, but you also have to comply with the "core curriculum" requirements. In other words, even if they accepted the full 120, you still had classes to take. The core curriculum requirements are essentially four or five classes you have to take from different groups. There's the biology group, the science group, the literature, or the arts group, etc. I don't recall them all. It was 4 or 5 classes, so roughly around 18 credits.

Overall, I had to take 48 credits to get my bachelor's degree in philosophy. Law school only starts each August. August 2007 was not an option. August 2008 was tight but doable. I did all in my power to make it for the 2008 law class. I had three semesters and a summer to take 48 credits, the LSAT, the TOEFL, and to do the law school application which is quite a bit of work too. I would max up my semester credits at 15, when possible, because sometimes the classes you need are not available. At the same time, I continued working at Key Control, even doing overtime regularly. Eli was very accommodating. He would let me go to classes during the day if I had to. I am forever thankful to how understanding he was. I've lost touch with him. Maybe he'll read this book.

The hardest thing was the LSAT. I enrolled in a Kaplan course to train for it. I had heard it was hard. I (forever arrogant) was not intimidated at all. "It must be hard for normal people" I'd think, not for me. Little did I know, the LSAT was *really* hard. I took my first practice test, and I scored like a 137. I was scoring the lowest—or one of the lowest—in the Kaplan class. I couldn't believe it. I felt the dumbest I've ever felt. A 137 would have gotten me in no law school, let alone, FIU, the one I wanted to get into. Later I would understand that I wasn't really that dumb. The LSAT is essentially a speed-reading comprehension test. In 2007, though my English level was decent, I could not read English at the pace needed to score 153 in the LSAT. I had to find a solution. How do I make myself a superfast reader in such a short time? Believe it or not, my first decision was to quit the Kaplan course—which I had already paid in full. I don't think a normal person scoring as low as I was would have done this. But to me it made sense. None of the questions in the LSAT were rocket science or required pre-acquired knowledge. If they gave me 24 hours, I'd ace the test. But I only had 3 hours. I thought that what I needed was practice, not go to classes. I was already registered to take the LSAT late 2007, so I didn't have a lot of time to practice. I went for it anyway and I scored around 148. A little better, but still not enough to get into FIU Law.

I already had submitted my application to FIU Law. They told me that I could get in as long as I got a higher LSAT score, 150+ they told me. The commitment to FIU made me take the test more seriously. The LSAT scoring system is very complicated. Going up two points can be a mission. But I was committed. I took maybe just 12 credits that semester, bought a hundred practice tests. I knew exactly what I needed to do: practice, practice, practice. And I did. I would take a couple of 35-min. test sections before clocking in at Key Control, a couple at lunch, and a couple after work/classes. My averages started improving. I also was more strategic. I knew for example that I couldn't possibly get through all 4 sections of the reading comprehension section. I simply wasn't fast enough. So, I decided to skip one. I would complete three as best as I could, trying to get all answers correct, and the last one, I'd mark it at random, which would also give me one or two out of seven correct answers, based on plain probability. If I mark all B, it's impossible I don't get one or two out of seven, I thought. This was a better strategy. I needed to get 21 plus (out of 28) in each section in order to get the score I needed. Spending more time in three sections—and not missing—was a better deal than rushing through four and being imprecise in the answers. It worked. In the end, I scored around 157. I don't remember exactly. What I do remember is that it was way more than the 150 the FIU Law admissions lady had told me about. I was going to get admitted. All I needed was to get the bachelor's degree which I would finish in May 2008. (Between you and me, bachelor's level classes at FIU, and I think in the U.S., are very easy. There was no concern there.).

Though I was very excited to go to law school, I was not per se in love with "law." The excitement was more connected with the achievement. Getting admitted to law school, specially a decent one, for me, a Peruvian immigrant, was a big deal. There was also some prestige to it. "I am going to law school" was received with a bit of a "wow" reaction.

Law school had me with mixed feelings, good and bad. On the good side, certain classes were intellectually challenging, way more than at the bachelor's level. Intellectual challenge turns me on. It was exciting. I remember being so excited at my Contracts class with Professor Gabilondo and being fascinated, almost philosophizing, by the nature of contracts, what makes them binding, why the law protects them, etc. Same with Constitutional Law.

I remember being fascinated while reading all these incredibly logical and well-reasoned Supreme Court opinions. It was delightful, intellectually. On the other side, I hated legal research and writing. On legal research, I was simply not very good at it, and nobody likes things one is not very good at. On legal writing, I simply couldn't get it. Coming from a philosophy background where you write reasoned opinions about other opinions, legal writing did not make sense. It was to me like copy and paste. You just had to find citations, organize them, and make them sound like a coherent sentence. It was all so tight and with so little freedom; plus, I was not very good at it. I scored low on writing classes. I am still not very good, 12 years later, but I have come to love it. I think legal writing, when done well, is fascinating. It has the strong logical foundations of philosophy; it's just limited on the things you can say—the citations, the law, the precedent. It has its beauty.

I went through law school without loving it and believing simply that I had to get good enough grades so I could get a decent paying job after it—and I did. I graduated in the top 25% of a very competitive class. This was remarkable considering my limited English skills which limited me on all the writing classes. Little did I know, grades are not everything …

Then came the Florida Bar exam. The Florida Bar exam, I must say, is by far the hardest exam I've taken. Two days, 12 hours, endless topics. I studied two months nonstop for it. I did not work during my Florida Bar exam prep. It was such a massive undertaking that the idea of failing and having to take it again made me panic. That made me, at the same time, put in as much effort as possible. I would study 8 hours per day, 6 days per week. I would do 8 hours of what I called "pure study." In short, I would put my timer for two-hour sessions, and then take breaks of anywhere between 15 minutes to two hours. It would take me between 10 to 12 hours to complete my 8 hours of "pure study." My 8 hours of "pure study" was way more than a lot of the law school kids' "15 hours" study days, I am sure. When my timer was on, I was all business. No phone, no talk, no nothing. Pure concentration. In the end, I passed the Florida Bar exam, by a decent margin. I had already completed the character and fitness part of the Florida Bar application and had my approval. Soon after I got my results, I was admitted to the Florida Bar as an attorney. One of my biggest achievements. Something I am incredible proud of. I wish my mother had been here to see it.

* * *

It was July 2011, and we as a country were still experiencing the impact of the Great Recession. During law school, I did not know what I wanted to practice nor was I hyper enthusiastic about "the law" like I mentioned earlier. I applied to several firms right after I took the bar exam and was waiting for my results. One firm, Rivero, gave me an opportunity to work doing in-house document review for a big case it was handling where they were defending several directors of a big, failed Puerto Rican bank. I was paid $25 an hour, and I was paid for as many hours as I did. Some weeks even more than 40 hours. At the time, it wasn't a bad job. Few of my former classmates had jobs. I at least was reviewing documents and getting paid.

Once I passed the bar, I continued to work at Rivero as an "attorney" but essentially doing the same—reviewing documents. Gradually, they started assigning me projects like draft discovery, simple motions, or research. Though a medium size law firm, it represented big corporations, and the work was "big law"[1] type of work. Any motion would go through 100 edits, and what you originally wrote, by the time it was filed, was virtually unrecognizable. Besides the natural effect to your pride of seeing your work literally destroyed by three layers of supervising attorneys, I did not find the modus operandi efficient. Writing is an art that carries a lot of subjectivity in it. And if you assign three attorneys to edit a document, the original work will always be unrecognizable in the end; you might as well give it to the final attorney to write it to begin with.

The focus on form rather than substance or ideas was one of the very first things I disliked about working for Rivero. In my mind, substance should be the priority. I thought to myself, if I ever practice on my own, I will never prioritize form over substance. Sure, documents should not have typos or improper sentences—that we can all agree on—but I was convinced that ideas and rock-solid logic and analysis win cases, not commas, semicolons, or periods. Do not misunderstand my words though, I am no advocate for typos or sloppy writing. My team knows better to present me pristine, spotless briefs. There is no reason whatsoever why briefs should have avoidable mistakes like typos. Our emphasis

---

[1] In our industry, we colloquially refer to "big law" as practicing in the big law firms defending large corporations and making big salaries.

though, again, is not on form, but substance, and rock-solid analysis and application of the law. Nobody in my firm gets yelled at for a typo.

Of the five document reviewers that started with me at Rivero, only three were offered permanent associate attorney positions after we passed the bar. I only learned of this later when the rumor circulated and then some of them confirmed it to me. The other two, we were not offered a job but continued to do whatever was assigned on an hourly basis, mostly document review. This meant that in weeks where there was no actual work, we could end up working only 20 hours; and getting paid just 20 hours. No benefits, no stability. Thus, as soon as I learned I was not among the "chosen ones," proud as I've always been, I started searching for other jobs. In my proud mind, "how are they going to offer a job to X or Y and not me?" I did not feel that the three lawyers chosen were particularly more talented or better than me. Worse yet, I felt that—at least one of them—sucked completely. In other words, I was offended.

I landed an interview at a large firm called Vernis and Bowling (Vernis) to do insurance defense. Vernis offered me $60,000 a year. This was October 2012. The salary was higher than Rivero, the position was stable, and I would get my own office (we were working at folding tables; and later at 4x2 feet cubicles at Rivero).[2] The workload promised to be heavy, as I was told that my "billable" hour requirement was 55 hours per week. But I was one that never had issue with too many hours, or too much work. I would trade that for the income any day, twice on Sunday.

---

[2] Ever since my experience working at folding tables, I promised myself that, when I had a firm, not even my paralegals would work at folding tables or 4 feet cubicle-desks.

If Rivero was unfulfilling or frustrating, Vernis was hell. While at Rivero we prepared long high-quality documents, at Vernis my boss would yell at me when I took too long writing something or when I wrote a motion from scratch rather than just using the firm's template and changing names. Insurance defense was, at least in my short experience at Vernis, a legal factory. Results secondary to winning; billing takes priority. Of course, I am not one to pass judgment on Vernis; maybe they are a good firm. My experience might have been tainted by having a bad boss—whom I know is no longer there. Let's call him Carlos.

I had two major arguments with Carlos. One of them I don't remember what it was about exactly. What I remember is that when I left Carlos' office into the paralegal cubicle area, several of the paralegals asked me: "You weren't fired?" Nope, I said. They were surprised to hear him yelling at me, and then me yelling back at him, and that I was not fired. The second argument was about a case. I did not want to make the argument he wanted me to; I didn't find a basis for it. It seemed frivolous to me. We argued, he yelled, I yelled back. I left his office. A couple of days later it was the end of my 90-day probationary period. Carlos summoned me to his office and told me what I expected to hear, that I was not going to be working there any longer beyond those 90 days.

Though sad, I was, in many ways, relieved.

1.2. Ayala Law, P.A.

Although I was not unhappy of leaving Vernis, I was afraid. Once again, for the third time in my life, I had to start back at zero. Not at "zero" zero, because I think I had about $5,000 in my bank account, but from scratch. My biggest concern was my expenses and student debt. I managed to get another deferment of the student debt. I was relieved from that for the moment.

I had just rented out a house I had purchased by the FIU Law campus. When I worked at Rivero, I decided that the drive was too long, so I rented a small studio in Le Jeune Road for $780 a month. The rental income covered my mortgage. I just needed to cover my $780 rent, gas, and food. I had no girlfriend, so that's quite some savings too.

What do I do now? — I asked myself.

I spent 48 hours thinking and building the courage to venture and do what I really wanted, to start my own law firm. I knew nothing about building a firm. I had no clients. I knew nothing as far as a particular area of law I could sell to the public as a product. I had not learned litigation defense during the year I was at Rivero or in the three months at Vernis.

1.3. Juan Carlos Gomez

Somewhere within these 48 hours, I spoke to Juan Carlos Gomez. Juan Carlos Gomez was my immigration law professor at FIU Law. Juan Carlos is literally an angel from heaven. Words are not enough to describe Juan Carlos. Juan Carlos is the best of humanity all in one, a beacon of hope. He has a heart that does not fit well within his body. Juan Carlos cares, he cares too much.

From my very first sessions at FIU Law's Immigration Clinic, Juan Carlos struck me as a humble guy with intellectual talent higher than what you see in a humble personality like his. Juan Carlos is your messy, super smart guy with a gigantic memory, who never takes notes. He would cite the immigration code off the top of his head. Never took notes for class. Never had notes of his class. But he didn't have to. Everything he knows is in his head. I remember how we, law students, in charge of six to eight pro bono matters at the Immigration Clinic, couldn't keep tract of our own cases well, while Juan Carlos knew every single one of our cases better than ourselves. That multiplied times ten or twelve students. That also, on top of the cases in his own practice. I simply couldn't understand how a human being could remember so much. Later, to a different level, while running my own practice, and knowing the firm's cases at times better than some in my team who handle a fraction of the ones I am in charge of, I learned that it is part memory, and part care. When you care, you don't forget things.

Over the years, Juan Carlos has become a very important part of my life. He's saved me during countless emotional meltdowns, legal conundrums, or ethical matters. He's simply been there for me when it mattered the most, notwithstanding his extremely busy schedule.[3]

Going back to the decisive 48 hours of reckoning, my conversation with Juan Carlos was key. I opened up about my sense of frustration and failure at being fired. I shared my frustration and the uncertainty I felt about the legal field. I shared with him my fear of the future. But I recall one day when I was in one of his immigration classes at the clinic, he told us: Hey, learn this, this will help you take real cases, and if one day you need to hang out your shingle, you'll have something. I told him about what he told us. And I sort of wanted his blessing and support to go on my own.

He encouraged me to go on my own with full strength. He thought I had what it took, and that I would do great things. He told me to take on immigration cases and that he'd help me out if I didn't know how to

---

[3] On a different note, I've asked him to be my partner many times, but he's always refused, saying he's not a good partner and he'd ruin my firm. It is not true, but I respect his opinion.

handle them. As if his generosity weren't immense already, he offered me to go to Krome Detention Center in Miami, on leads he would give me, do the intake interview, and if the client signed in, we'd split the fee. An immensely generous deal given that he provided the lead (and the knowledge), and I brought little to the table. I could have simply been his paralegal if you factor the equities.

One thing is for sure and that is Juan Carlos brought me over the top in terms of the hesitancy I felt as to what I had to do. Forty-eight hours after leaving Vernis, I started Ayala Law, P.A. from my studio in Le Jeune Road. I went on Sunbiz.org and I incorporated the entity. One of the most fascinating adventures of my life had started. I was scared, but I was committed.

1.4. The Beginnings

In early 2013, I was still not passionate about the law. I did not love it. I did not hate it either. If you are reading this and feel similarly, know that this is also part of a personality problem. Some of us simply like too many things and cannot really be good or focused on just one thing. For me, it is virtually impossible. I was never the guy who "always wanted to be a lawyer since I was 12." I ended up choosing law first because I thought I could do it. I had recently obtained my first work permit (after almost four years undocumented in the U.S.) and the first thing I wanted to do is go to school. It had always been a dream of mine since I was a child to go to school in the U.S., as I mentioned earlier.

But back to the beginnings of Ayala Law. Though I was not in love with the law in 2013, this time it felt a little different. I had this little baby called Ayala Law, P.A. that I had to nurture and grow. And I did not only have to baby it as a general goal or mission; if it did not work out,

I would not eat, simple as that. There was the immediate direct pressure of making a living through Ayala Law, or else, go back to a Rivero or Vernis type of place. That alone was a huge motivator. Further, if Ayala Law failed, it was exclusively because of me. I could not blame a partner, or an employer—nobody.

Ayala Law made me marry the law in a stronger way. I was not only going to keep sticking to the law as a personal mission of this forever distracted and unfocused person, but it was also now the product my company sold. In a way, it made my personal life commitment to the law a little easier. If I were to succeed, I had to polish my product: the knowledge of the law and my legal skills.

I had to figure out exactly what I was going to sell though. I had a partial answer to that question: immigration. Good soul Juan Carlos would help me out (subject to his time limitations) if I ran into trouble in cases.

Then, I needed to figure out how to sell it and to whom. I had no idea about marketing, and I hated networking to no end. I was simply not born for small talk. From the inception, it was clear that my personality was not a good fit for business. I was not a natural at it from a pure personality standpoint. I hated people. I am the type of guy who goes into the elevator and pushes the close door button fast to make sure the person a few feet behind do not get in with me. Misanthropic, I've called myself sometimes, though the term may be a little radical.

I had to figure out also what I was going to eat until I found a regular stream of income. I remember going to Flagler Street, to one of those by-the-pound food places. They had a "cantina" deal, where they sell you weekly meals for about $25 dollars. I could eat the cantina daily meals for lunch and dinner. So, my lunch expenses were controlled at

$25 per week. For breakfast, McDonald's or Burger King for about $5 at a time. But living this cheap was not viable. As a 34-year-old, I needed some distraction and go out with friends occasionally (it was also a good business practice to go out and talk to people—unbeknownst to then Eduardo).

I created a Facebook and LinkedIn page. I went on Craigslist to see if I could find supplemental income. I found "coverage" lawyer opportunities, where you go cover a hearing for another lawyer for anywhere between $75 to $150 per hearing. I also posted ads on Craigslist offering not only immigration services but litigation. Though I had no idea how to litigate, I had done a bit of it at Rivero and Vernis and, typical me, I offered it without knowing exactly how to do it. I'll figure the rest later, I thought. How hard can it be? I've always had this feeling that all things come down to basic principles.

That nothing, nothing is complicated *per se*. It is partially a byproduct of my philosophical background and "philosophy is the mother of all sciences" type of approach. I know "the science," I thought, and all flows from there. Partially true, of course, a misapplication by me— later I'll learn. To practice a field, you need to know your stuff, or you can run into trouble. Of course, some figuring-out skills will get you around, but the most skillful problem solvers, in certain areas, will still fail without background in the area.

Back to the law firm. I went to a website that allows you to design one on your own and I created one myself at no cost. My brother-in-law, who had some artistic talent, helped me design a logo. That original logo and colors are still the basis of our current logo, which was redesigned by my good friend from high school, Kurt Gastulo, who has built a successful digital advertising company called Plan B.

First Ayala Law official logo

Seeking assistance here and there, finding free things here and there, I managed to start Ayala Law with virtually no dollars and save my little 5K savings for my expenses, and to survive for about six months, was my estimate. I did have to buy a printer in Office Depot for about $200 dollars. Back in the day, we printed a lot more than we do now, and a printer was a must.

From my deal with Juan Carlos, I got three or four cases. Later we took on more cases without pay or that were supposed to pay but never paid. Collection in immigration is a huge challenge. But Juan Carlos is like that. He just likes to help people more than he can control. I am a little bit like that too, with a touch more business-sense. I'll trade his heart for my business-sense in an instance though.

My half of the cases I took with Juan Carlos was a hefty fee for me then that helped keep going. But regardless of the number of paid cases I took in these first months or years, the most important thing I obtained during these beginnings was that I learned immigration at a high level. I learned removal defense, virtually all type of family petitions, and became well versed in immigration law. I understood the Immigration and Nationality Act and the internal logic of the law. Immigration is a unique field that is sort of like a language. You "speak" immigration.

This knowledge, in turn, became the main practice area of my nascent firm and whenever I promoted my firm, I promoted immigration. At one point, I redesigned my website to be solely focused on immigration. Ayala Law, the immigration firm. This, I would learn later, is something practitioners need to be cautious about. What you market in your beginnings, will stick forever. Today, though immigration is about 20% of what we do, a lot of people still think of Eduardo as an immigration lawyer only rather than a litigator, my main area of practice today.

I also took on some commercial cases. From Craigslist, I got my first litigation case. A man named Alex, a Canadian Iranian guy on his mid-thirties who lived the good life in his Miami Beach condo and his Lamborghini. I still don't know well where his money came from, but back then, I was not too good at due diligence type of stuff. I needed the money, so I took the case. In my defense, he did not appear to me to be a bad person. I am still thankful to him because, being a nobody, having no office, and him knowing that I was a new second-year lawyer, he did not mind hiring me. The fact he was super cheap and did not want to pay a more established lawyer, might have helped too.

Alex had a problem with his condo association. He had undertaken a full remodeling of his unit, had submitted all his permit work and plans to the condo board, gotten it approved by Miami Beach, but the board was still giving him a hard time about some impact windows he wanted to install in his unit and that were part of the plans submitted and approved by the same condo board. The already purchased windows, the re-design (if he had to), and the additional labor would have cost Alex more than 10 thousand dollars. Alex could pay for the adjustments, but (1) he was very cheap, and (2) he felt he was on the right (he was) since he relied on what he had submitted to the association (and was approved by them) to undertake his work. The fact the board overlooked the design should not be his fault. Litigious as he is, he had me sue them. Without knowing much about these types of cases, not having tried a case in my life (or nearly gotten to the final pretrial stages of cases), I drafted a complaint and sued an important Miami Beach condo association. Though I did not know what I was doing, I thought that if I filed a complaint, send some discovery, it would burden the association with legal fees and push them to settle. I was wrong about that (I'll learn later in life), but I got lucky in this instance as the association, who hired a good firm, quickly settled to get rid of me and Alex for an amount that was satisfactory to Alex, who had merely paid me about $1,500 to sue them. The success in this case gave me the wrong impression of litigation and its gigantic complexities and risks. With this misperception, I would later sign onto litigation cases where I would struggle highly.

1.5. Office

A few months into my Le Jeune studio law firm, I decided I needed office space. If I was going to meet potential clients, I needed a conference room. I was now making about $4,000 net in revenue, which covered my expenses and left me some extra. I looked into virtual office spaces. I rented my first office space at 900 Biscayne. A virtual office space where I could have a legal address and get mail. For about $150 a month, I could also use their conference room for 4 or 5 hours. I had my office at 900 Biscayne for a few months but did not use it much. I was still doing all my work from the Le Jeune studio.

Then came, via Juan Carlos, another business opportunity. Juan Carlos was friends with John De Maria, a charismatic lawyer in his late 50s or early 60s. John De Maria was good at bringing cases. He ran, for the most part, a personal injury and civil rights practice, but had contacts with several consulates where a lot of immigration leads come from. Seeing the potential, John talked to Juan Carlos to get into a deal to take on immigration cases and split the fee. Juan Carlos didn't have the time between teaching and his practice, so I, desperate for business, immediately volunteered when he told me about it.

I met John De Maria in his office near Sunset Place Mall in South Miami. A 2,000 square feet nice office space with about five people working in it. The deal offered to me was: he brings the cases, we sign them under his firm's name, he provides the staff, office, supplies, mail, etc. I work on the cases as the lawyer. The split, 50/50. Back then, it seemed like an OK deal to me. When I had no busy practice, the deal worked well since I did not mind taking less than my fair share of the fee.

During my first year in Ayala Law, and in part of my second year, I would sign up for document review (doc review, as we call it) projects as an independent contractor to supplement my income. Doc review is what I did before at Rivero, but at a larger scale. These are companies that all they do is review documents. It's a huge business. Large firms in super large antitrust, commercial, or class action cases are faced with millions and millions of documents they have to review. Big Law usually don't have the stuff or business infrastructure to have lawyers review all these documents. Doc review companies, in turn, who pay between 20 to 30 dollars an hour to a licensed lawyer, have created an entire business model over this need and can provide the service at economical rates ($150, $200 an hour), which is cheap for big law rates usually north of $600 an hour.

The doc review projects I did would pay me between 21 to 28 dollars an hour on the better projects. Most doc review companies allowed you flexibility, meaning that you could do your own thing on the side if you wanted, no conflict of interest or issues with liability policies. Some forced you to a minimum of hours while others allowed you to do as many or as little as you wanted. Depending on the time or the type of project I was in, I would work on average 30 to 40 hours per week. My schedule would go like this: start working at 6:30 a.m. until like 3:00 p.m. in my firm, and right after that go to doc review at 4:00 p.m. until 10:00 p.m. Some weeks I did doc review on Saturdays too. If hours were offered, I volunteered. Working this many hours while my firm was already starting to provide some income, allowed me to virtually keep all the doc review income to then reinvest it in the firm.

I was a little embarrassed to do doc review. At doc review sites, it almost feels like you have the lawyers that have not been able to make it in a real practice. I'd say 80% of the lawyers in doc review felt like me. There were some older lawyers who had lost jobs or their practices and were at doc review. Lawyers who had tried hundreds of cases, now reviewing documents. I always felt a sense of shame when I would tell others that I had my practice while at doc review. If I had my practice and I was doing doc review, it obviously meant my practice was not succeeding. Not sure if people saw it like that. But that's what my negative self would think. In any event, regardless of how I felt, I had to disclose that I had my practice at doc review because it was full of lawyers who were a gold mine for potential referral of cases. Lawyers traditionally have been.

Going back to De Maria, I started doing intakes on his leads and taking cases at his Sunset Place office. At the beginning, I was using one of his empty offices. Soon after, I had to leave the office because he needed it. Once I left that office, which I used for a few weeks, the deal became not so good to me. I had to do all the cases from my own space and did not have the benefit of using his support staff to work on the cases. I was not happy.

At De Maria's office I met Abby. If I was 35, Abby was probably 23 or 24. Abby is an immigrant from Central America. She had been in the U.S. since childhood on TPS (Temporary Protected Status). Abby was one of the brightest young women I've ever met. Abby *was* John De Maria's firm. John, more of a salesman than a lawyer, charismatic but unorganized, was entirely dependent on Abby. Abby would do pre-suit, pretrial work, discovery, letter writing, client managing. Abby would do it all. Abby was sweet and did not mind my sometimes irreverent, unconventional style. Abby was hardworking—as most immigrants— and I am sure she did at De Maria's firm more than she should, or more than whatever rate she was making merited. When I started my deal with De Maria, she helped me with the immigration cases. She would ask me things because she thought I should know immigration, but in reality, I was fairly lost in many cases, and she would actually be better situated than me to answer these questions. I would defer for later her questions when I didn't know the answer to a question that needed to be answered in order to be able to sign a client. I would tell her that I'd "research" it (i.e., text Juan Carlos. I tell you, Juan Carlos, is gold).

Later, she would go on to get married, go to law school, and form a family up in the north part of Florida. When she graduated from law school, where I am confident, she excelled, I offered her to work together, but she was at a different stage in her life (she had given birth to a baby), and very far geographically.

Not too long after my initial deal with De Maria (I'd say less than 6 months), he moved offices to Brickell, in the same building where the

Mexican consulate is, where he had good connections too. The move was strategic. A lot of leads came from the Mexican consulate. When De Maria moved to Brickell, I still took cases with him on our 50/50 deal. But the deal had become less attractive to me. Most immigration cases are flat fee cases. On a case where you charge $4,000, I would only take $2,000. The case then would last 5 to 6 years and the $2,000 are long gone in the past. In fact, I still have some cases from those times, cases that have not paid a dollar in more than six years, and that we cover, virtually pro bono.

I did not want to break my relationship with John De Maria. I found him to be a well-connected guy. But my practice had grown a bit, and I had the supplemental income from doc review. So, I decided that I needed my first physical office. I could no longer work off of Le Jeune and it was already *de facto* understood that John did not have to provide an office under our deal—nor did I want it from him by then. I asked John to rent one office inside his office. That way I would feel the freedom to take as much of my own cases without the pressure of having to take cases with him—I would be a tenant now; I could do as I saw fit with my cases. Our deal would stay on, but I would turn down a lot more cases, given that they were not very profitable to me. I would run my own practice from an office in his practice for about $900 a month—all included. It was a tiny office in Brickell, with no windows, but it was *my* own office. My *first* office ever. Neither Rivero nor Vernis had given me my own office. Ayala Law (or myself) gave me my first office.

I had always wanted an office. It was sort of a dream of mine. I thought it was cool to have an office. To say, "I am going to my office." "Stop by my office." It felt executive, important. The former Dunkin' Donuts,

Publix Supermarkets guy, had his own office as an attorney in the best country in the world. I was proud, and the people that loved me were proud too.

My first office inside De Maria's office. It had not windows.

Photo from September 2014

Having a physical office felt, in a way, like the real start of the firm. Before a physical location, the firm almost feels like you are a freelancer. With an office, a phone, rent, and office supplies, it starts to feel like a real business. Even today, the business is highly anthropomorphic (the business is me); but as it grows and adds personnel, and these humans bring their talent and input into the firm, Eduardo fades and the business becomes its own entity and soul, a combination of the talents of the group.

Though some months I would not know where the hell I would cover my expenses from, cases always came in the most unexpected ways. Talking to the barber who had a brother who wanted to come from his country; talking to a server at a restaurant who needed a renewal of a work permit; reconnecting with contacts from high school in Peru who were now businessmen and had business connections with the U.S. and needed legal work here, you name it. Cases simply appeared from under the table, in the most unexpected ways. As long as I was alive, talking to people, doing good work on current cases, more cases would come.

As the firm grew in revenue, it was much harder for me to do doc review. And as much as I did not want to let go of that safe, easy income, I had to if the firm was going to continue growing. Sometime in the second year of Ayala Law, I stopped it. Leaving doc review, while it created a sort of insecurity in terms of the income situation, was also a moment to be proud.

I could finally live out of the revenues of my own firm, which had a little structure also: an office, website, systems, templates, etc. The business formalities. I would no longer have to go to doc review to click on boxes with a mouse. Leaving doc review, in a way, was liberating. Plus, God, I was leaving one the most boring jobs in the world ever!

Around that time also, I realized that I was doing too much non-legal, clerical work that could be done by somebody else at a much lower rate. I needed an assistant. But if I hire an assistant, where am I going to put him/her? I needed another office. I talked to John. He had the office next to me, even smaller than mine, empty. For $700 extra, I rented from him that additional space. I went to Craigslist, and I bought two used 5x5 cubicles, which I installed in the new office. One for my new assistant, and one for a potential future assistant. The firm was starting to take shape.

First set of cubicles – Photo from September 2014

But I disliked my association with John De Maria more and more. We had different philosophies about how to practice law, to put it mildly. More bluntly, he was a gigantic mess. His firm was a mess. His cases were a mess. I did not know how you could live stress free without having a good handle on your case load: what deadlines are coming, what filings had to be done, what cases are pending, etc. Moreover, the office had his name and logo at the front, and everyone that came in thought I was a John De Maria associate. I hated that because I did not want to be associated with a practice that I thought was a mess. I also had been working so hard to build the name Ayala Law for it to be diluted or confused with a name I did not want to be associated with. It was time to go.

1.6. The Florida Bar

During the early years of my practice, I started to meet several small business owners and taking on business transactions and commercial litigation cases—both things I did not know well, but as usual, unafraid, and unaware, I took on the cases. The income pressure was also high, and I simply couldn't afford to turn down business.

Litigation is an ugly beast; when you know what you are doing. When you don't, it is a massive monster that can destroy you. In litigation, you are always in the middle of a conflict between two parties that hate each other enough to be able to file and defend (and pay for) a legal proceeding. Behind the parties, there are usually two attorneys whose livelihood is better if the case prolongs. As much as an attorney may in good conscience try to settle or shorten the matter for the benefit of the legal system, the client, or plain justice, the longer and more intense it is, the more the lawyer makes in income. It is an unavoidable fact of litigation that will always be one of the factors driving it to one extent or another. The lawyer's relationship with his client is better the more he destroys his case and vice versa; an inevitable zero-sum game. Add lawyers' complex personalities, pride, and usually intricate intellects, and you have a gigantic nasty mess. All these things turn lawyering into a stressful profession.

Though I got around the handful of litigation cases that I took then, there was one case that went a little out of control for me, a neophyte to the industry. In retrospect, with the experience I have now, the case was not complex at all. It was a simple commercial case involving fraud where there was maybe three or four hundred thousand at stake—literally, an average case for the Ayala Law of today. Back then, it was a massive case for me. I took the case, erroneously, in exchange for a ten thousand deposit and, after that, on contingency. But here is the thing, John De Maria brought the case, so he took *five thousand dollars* just for introducing me to the guy. It was a very bad deal. Today, we wouldn't take such a case on a pure contingency basis. And if it was a bad deal already, imagine how bad a deal it was after having to hand John half of the fee?

The defendant was a straight up crook. The type of guy I deal with in most of my litigation cases today. He hired a seasoned defense lawyer. One of those guys with 25 plus years of experience, in his early fifties, who lived at 73 West Flagler (the Miami-Dade County Court) day in and day out. In the world of litigation, there are two main types of attorneys from the standpoint of where they practice: the state court guys and the federal court guys. The state court guys are generally guys with a lot of familiarity with state court rules, and the ins and outs of the court. Judges know them by name because they are there every day. They are usually eloquent, talkative, articulate, orally persuasive, charismatic. Some of them also know how things should be done by the book, and how much they can get away straying out from ethics and other rules without getting per se in trouble. The federal guys are different; more intellectual. They may have oral skills as well, but they are in essence fantastic briefers. Guys with more intellectual power who can persuade the likewise higher intellect of federal court judges via paper.

My opposing counsel was the typical state court guy, knowledgeable of the state court system, and unconcerned with ethics, so long as he didn't get in trouble. That's the line some lawyers walk, the license line so to speak.

I ventured in the drafting process. I drafted a long complaint with the long set of facts described to me by the client. I sued the defendant for 19 different causes of action. Back then, my logic was: the more, the better, no? Today, we have a more balanced approach. We pick three to five solid causes of actions to avoid demanding motion writing in the fight past motions to dismiss. At the end of the day, all you need is one cause of action and win on it.

So, I filed my complaint, and tried to serve it on the defendant and his corporation—which was himself, he was the corporation. The guy had two luxurious apartments in Brickell and an office in Doral. I sent my process server to each location multiple times, but the guy was intentionally avoiding service. He would instruct receptionists to tell the process server that he did not live there. I did not know what to do. Today, after ten years of litigation experience, I know quite a bit of the jurisprudence on service of process, and I could see me doing so many things differently. Back then, I did not know any better. Antisocial as I was, I did not have many other lawyers to call and ask for advice. I did not have a litigation mentor either.

In conversations with my clients (two brothers), it came out that they had a copy of the defendant's passport. This is not unusual in cases of business partnerships gone sour. My clients and defendants were intimately close at one point and one of the brothers, aiding his former friend to get a visa to the UAE, had gotten the defendant's passport. In an unrelated conversation, my client asked me if we could know where the defendant was based on immigration records, and I told him that was impossible. That you would need to have his passport at a minimum. We have it!—they said. Oh well, I'll see what I can do, I said.

At that time, ninety percent of my cases were immigration cases, between deportation and visa petitions cases. In immigration cases, it is routine that you get the clients' travel record online. It is an automatic thing to do. Most applications require what's called an I-94 and travel history. At the CBP website you would fill an online form, click some buttons, and bam, you had your client's record of travel to the U.S. One of these clicks is a button where you swear under penalty of perjury that you are either the person, a guardian of the person, or that you otherwise have authority to get the person's record.

In your practice, you always have the consent of your client based on the contract for representation with your client. A different situation is when you are seeking the travel record of a defendant or an adverse party. You clearly don't have consent. But the process was so mechanic and routine for us, that I (or my assistant) must have looked for the defendant's travel record, clicked that we had consent, without even thinking, when we did not have consent. This may seem like a small, harmless error; after all, the crook defendant was intentionally avoiding the lawsuit after having already defrauded my client by hundreds of thousands of dollars.

As it turns out, it was not. Later in the case, after some motion filing and hearings, opposing lawyer learned of my trick. How did he learn? Through none other than my client! My client, who still talked to the defendant (clients do that despite you telling them not to talk to defendants) emailed the defendant saying something like this: "My attorney has a lot of contacts with immigration and he's able to obtain your immigration record. We are going to get you sooner or later." In the same email, he attached an email from me to him forwarding the defendant's travel record.

In the middle of contentious litigation, a nasty relationship with opposing counsel, and just having lost on defendant's motion to compel arbitration on some aspects of the case, I receive an official letter from The Florida Bar. This was my second or beginning of my third year as a lawyer. Official communications from The Florida Bar are the last thing you want to get. This was actually my second. Before, I had already received one with a complaint from an adverse party (someone I did not represent and whom I advised of multiple times). The complaint essentially said that I failed to explain to him my limited role in the transaction (as escrow agent) and that I did not represent him. When the transaction went south, he tried to go after me by filing a bar complaint. But I had taken extreme measures to assure I was protected, and that I had no say in the transaction *per se*, as an advisor, but just as a recipient of some funds. I sent a letter to The Florida Bar explaining what had happened, showed them the emails and texts, and the complaint was quickly dismissed.

This second one was more troublesome. The defendant authored it, and in essence complained that I had illegally used his personal information to obtain his private travel records without having his consent. The complaint had merit; I did do that, albeit without intent. What was obvious to anyone that could read the complaint was that it was not filed by the defendant but by opposing lawyer in an effort to make me angry, get me in trouble with the Bar, perhaps withdraw from the case, but for sure, sidetrack my prosecution of the case with a needless and annoying distraction. This happens in litigation a lot. I call them "sideshows."

I didn't particularly like my client. The one brother leading the case was quite annoying, intense, and demanding. After he got me in trouble so he could brag about "his lawyer's connections with immigration," in an effort to intimidate the defendant who he shouldn't be talking to anyways, you could imagine how angry I was at him.

The Bar complaint was potentially serious, and I was not going to let even the slightest chance to jeopardize all I had in my life—my law license. The only thing I had ever achieved: to be a member of The Florida Bar and my ability to practice law. Not financially solvent, I had to hire an ethics lawyer—one of those lawyers who defend lawyers. Looking online, I found Kevin Tynan. Kevin Tynan is a fantastic attorney. Up to today, I have him on retainer as a permanent ethics advisor for me and my firm. Kevin is charismatic, knowledgeable, and highly experienced. Most importantly, Kevin will tell it to you like it is, in simple language; no sugar coating at all.

Kevin evaluated the case and told me that he believed I was not at risk of suspension. Given my newness to the Bar, the fact that it was unintentional, and that it was my first offense, it was unlikely I would get a suspension. He did think though that we should carefully defend the case. I prepared a long letter in response to the complaint that he then edited and sent to the Bar as my attorney. After we sent our response, a meeting was due with the local bar attorney in charge of my file. I met with the lawyer and Kevin at a law firm in Brickell. Kevin knew the lady, but most importantly, he was very familiar or had a professional relationship with the lady's boss up north. She asked me questions. I explained what happened, the context, and my lack of intent. I apologized sincerely for what I did. The meeting ended.

After that, Kevin took over. I'm not sure what happens behind the scenes, but it is sort of like a negotiation between the defense attorney and the prosecutor in criminal cases. After a while, Kevin told me that he had managed the prosecuting attorney to agree to me simply going to a one-day ethics class in Tallahassee. I would get no suspension, no public reprimand, and most importantly, my record would not show any disciplinary record—what mattered the most to me. Being a lawyer in the United States is my biggest professional achievement, and I wanted the respect of my peers. I felt that a disciplinary record would taint my reputation forever.

The Tallahassee ethics class was one of the most boring classes I've ever been to. Lawyers of all ages were there, most with a sense of shame for being there. As the class went on, during breaks, things got more relaxed, and it was not bad.

In parallel, and in consultation with Kevin, I decided this was a good opportunity to withdraw from the case. I told the client he had put me in an impossible position of potentially having to point the finger at him to defend myself for disclosing confidential emails. By then, we didn't have a good relationship and the case was not going well due to unethical lawyer's silly delaying tactics. Since John De Maria was also in the representation agreement, I told John he had to take it over because I had a conflict and, most importantly, irreconcilable differences with the client, whom I couldn't stand, and whom I hated for having disclosed confidential emails and putting my bar license at risk just because he wanted to brag to his former partner. Not to mention having to spend thousands of dollars in an ethics attorney. I was gone from the case. John, who knew even less about commercial litigation than me, took over the case. I am not sure what happened after that.

1.7. Bell's Palsy

The financial pressure, the sense of always being lost, the constant obligation to bring new cases, the stress that came from litigation, and the inherent confrontation with opposing counsels (which I did not know how to manage back then), all created a very stressful life I was not used to. Law school could get stressful during finals. The bar exam was stressful. But this lifestyle was a whole new level of stress.

One day, with my former wife at a pasta place in Brickell, Vapiano (now closed), we were in line waiting for our food and I tell her that I felt something weird in my lips and cheek. I felt like it was hardened. She looked at me and couldn't tell anything but noticed that my left eye was reddish in color. As I ate the pasta, I also felt weird, almost as if I couldn't feel the taste of it. We went about dinner and went home. At home, I looked at myself in the mirror, and I noticed that the left side of my face was not moving. It was now obvious to me that my left side was paralyzed. Other than the weirdness, the red eye, and some drooling, I did not feel that bad. I did not have a fever or a headache or massive discomfort.

I did not have insurance, so I called a doctor friend, and he told me that if my face was paralyzed, I needed to go to the emergency room right away, so I did. At the emergency room, I waited for like an hour, and then some doctors saw me. After a few tests, it was clear to the doctors that I had Bell's palsy. What is Bell's palsy? Nobody knows very well. According to Wikipedia, it is "a type of facial paralysis that results in a temporary inability to control the facial muscles on the affected side of the face." The doctor called it a "syndrome" and said it was unknown what could cause it. Stress could be one of the causes, he said.

Whether stress was the cause of my Bell's palsy or something else, I'll never know. But the fact is I was experiencing massive stress. After this,

I was seriously worried about the impact of the stress in my practice and my health. It was 2014, and, for the first time since I started law school in 2008—and my decision to stick to something I didn't like, the law—I started to question whether "sticking to it" was worthwhile.

I did not stop working though. I did not have much of a choice. I went to the office with paralysis and all, because, as I mentioned earlier, other than the uncomfortableness (it was annoying), I did not feel ill or lacking in energy. I did, though, make a commitment to myself that I was not going to stress more, or that I was going to manage my stress in a better way. If I failed at the law, or at the law firm project, that was secondary. I did not care anymore.

The thought of changing fields didn't cross my mind, it was only a little flirtation. The conclusion I came to was that I needed to diversify my income. On or around this time, I sold my first house and made around 70K in profit. I invested 60K of it in an insurance agency—one of the biggest business mistakes I've made. I cannot describe enough how stupid I was to pretend I could handle an insurance agency, and a nascent law firm, all at the same time. As you might expect, I failed miserably, and lost all my money, money that could have been better invested in my firm.

In any case, since the Bell's palsy time, I've been able to work with a "whatever happens, happens" type of attitude. Today, I handle, objectively, probably 10 times the amount of pressure that I had at the beginning, but I don't stress. To me, if things fall apart, they fall apart. I always work with a deep conviction that I leave it all in the field. If things failed, they likely did because of things beyond my control and so, why stress anyway? Moreover, today, I also practice more confident in my intellectual and legal skills. And that no matter what sanctions motions I face from unethical or evil opposing counsel, none of my cases is ever frivolous or without foundation.[4] That internal confidence has made me overcome incredibly malign challenges from lawyers and law firms who were literally out to destroy me, my client, and my firm. Litigation can be a nasty environment. And judges are no exception. Power, race, temper, personalities, play a huge role in the judiciary. More than the profession would like to admit.

1.8. 1390 Brickell

The second year, my firm went on to make $90,000 in net receipts. Probably $50,000 out of that was income for me after expenses. I had already been paying $1,600 in office space rent, so I felt comfortable paying that or perhaps up to $2,500 in rent so I could get a better office, one where my name was at the door. I could already see the potential for growth at Ayala Law, P.A., and I wanted a space where I could stay for a bunch of years and fit six to seven people at a minimum.

Back in 2014, I used to go to this workout bootcamp called Legacy Fit. At Legacy Fit, I met this late-twenties super handsome white guy—Jordan. Jordan was extremely fit and good looking. I don't recall how we started talking but sometime in between workouts we clicked and became friends. He told me he was a licensed attorney in Michigan, but that he "had other things going" in real estate. I thought he had a lot of businesses in real estate and that he was super wealthy. It turned out Jordan was just a good hard-working guy from up north that had

---

[4] We have also developed at the firm a good system to filter out cases. We turn down a lot of cases that are arguably meritorious but that will not withstand the brutal forces of litigation. Even then, especially in South Florida, defendants and its lawyers will paint your case as frivolous, fraudulent, or the like. You have to ignore this; otherwise, there really couldn't be any plaintiff lawyers out there.

decided to settle in Miami and was building his own brand as a high-end real estate agent, hustling along the way. Long story short, I contacted Jordan, and he started helping me to look for an office space.

He told me about this office down the street from John De Maria's office in Brickell Avenue and 14th Street. I didn't think I could afford much in Brickell, but I liked the idea of staying in Brickell, still close by John De Maria for potential business, and to make sure I checked my mail from my immigration cases.[5] The space was 900 square feet in a small five-story building owned and used by Pacific National Bank. The then tenant had just left middle of his lease, so the Bank had a good deal for me at around $2,900 a month, including 2 parking spaces. It was only me and my assistant, so I was good with two parking spaces.[6] The hard part was persuading my prospective landlord, the bank, that with $90,000 in revenues, I could afford this new rent. Though it was a struggle, I succeeded in persuading it, and signed a five-year lease. I had a new home.

I was super proud. The Dunkin' Donuts, Publix, heavy accent immigrant had its own law firm with a physical location in the heart of the Brickell Financial Center. It was a big deal to me. I also liked the fact that in that space I could fit, I thought, up to seven employees. How much will my payroll be by the time I have 7 employees? Whew, I thought, that's got to be a longggg time. Making payroll every two weeks was already hard, imagine a 7-employee payroll? It will be a long time I believed.

---

[5] In immigration cases, you can change your address 10 times, and government entities will still send you things to the address that you put in the initial filing.

[6] Since early on at my firm, I've always like to, within my means, take care of my employees. In Brickell, parking is a huge problem. You have big corporations like Bank of America who don't pay for their employees' parking. Ayala Law, P.A., as humble and poor as it was, paid for its employees' parking, always.

The move was not very hard. I had nothing. At John De Maria's office, I was using desks he had. So, I moved my papers and things and that was the move. I went to a furniture store in Hialeah and purchased two desks for the two offices, a small table for my conference room, and two used cubicles, one for my current assistant, and one for future ones. Early on, while we were still 2 or 3 people at the office, I rented the additional office space to a friend and client so he could run his business from there. Things changed when I had to hire an associate, a clerk, and another assistant. By the time we were five, the office started to feel crammed. Not even two years into it, and I could already see me not renewing my lease. It was time to plan.

1.9. Depression and Suits

On or around the time I moved into my new Brickell office, I experienced one of the worst breakups of my life. Not because it was traumatic, nasty, or aggressive. Quite the opposite. The woman I was with, whom I loved dearly, simply disappeared. One day to the next, she was simply gone. No goodbye talk, no calls, no texts—nothing. Someone I loved dearly, simply walked away without explanation. From one day to the next she became a stranger. It was, perhaps, worse than death. When someone dies, you have no options. They are simply gone. This was different. The person you loved was alive but wanted nothing with you—nothing at all—and you didn't know why. To know that she was alive but that by choice she simply did not want to even talk to you, was hard. I will never understand well the "why."

I was now in a life that combined a lot of law firm stress, long hours of work, financial insecurity, and to wrap it all up, emotionally broken. It was one of the toughest times of my life. And though I labeled this section "depression," I have to say that I was never diagnosed with depression or took any medication. In general, I am fairly stable emotionally—even in sadness. Killing myself or that kind of serious stuff are things that have never crossed my mind no matter how much I was crying of sadness in my bed. I have always been pragmatic. And killing yourself does not make any sense, pragmatically. Life is better than death, period.

I didn't know what to do. Other than perhaps sharing the sadness with a good friend—I am not the type that naturally seeks medical help. I didn't think I needed it. But the sadness was intense. For about three months I was destroyed inside, cried in my bed alone, and could not understand how a human being I cared so much about—and that used to say the same right back at me—did not care at all now. Until today, I can't think of what I did for her to depart. I do not know.

I took a practical approach to sadness. I said to myself, if I work a lot, and keep my mind occupied, I won't be able to think about it and I won't be sad. Of course, you can't entertain your head for all of the 18 hours or so that you are awake. But I had to try. Though I am a social drinker, I was never prone to alcoholism. Though I have tried drugs, there's something in me that never made me addicted. (Not liking it helps. I dislike the taste and smell of weed. Cocaine makes you feel like a chemical lab inside. I do not find any "pleasure" in it). I have experienced the intense feelings of several drugs I won't mention. But I have tried them—once or twice—and never in my life, did I feel that they were a threat to me. It's just not in me to be "addicted." From my pragmatic point of view, addiction makes no sense.

In my effort to keep my mind off sadness, I looked through Amazon Prime Video, and I found this show called Suits. Some of you reading probably know it very well. For those who don't, it was about lawyers, so it caught my interest. This section of the book is almost embarrassing to write, but Suits changed my life. It *literally* did. First it filled the rest of my "head-time" after I went from my Brickell office to my Brickell apartment alone, a block walk. I would eat something quick, and then watch Suits until I felt asleep. I simply loved Suits. I loved Harvey Specter and Mike Ross.

For those who haven't watched it, Harvey Specter is this big shot NYC attorney who always gets shit done and is the coolest dude. Good looking, well dressed, and smart, always has a way to get deals or cases done. He does it, passionate about the idea he has of himself that he's the best lawyer in the city—Manhattan. The best "closer," the rumor goes. He walks cool through the city, dates good looking women, lives in a fancy NYC apartment. He litigates aggressively and wins with passion and love; and a huge, fresh smile on his face. He was simply the coolest. Harvey though, is emotionally handicapped, incapable of commitment, and with unresolved family issues.

Mike Ross is younger. He gets a job as a lawyer in Harvey's firm by lying about being a lawyer to begin with. Mike was an intellectually brilliant kid with a fascinating memory who got sidetracked by hanging out with the wrong people but who always wanted to be a lawyer. Mike's parents were killed in a car accident when he was eleven and a mediocre lawyer got his grandma, who raised him, twenty grand as a settlement. Since then, he always wanted to be a lawyer. Harvey, who was impressed by Mike's brain and knowledge, despite not being a lawyer, hires him anyway to work as a lawyer. They start working together on cases, with Mike taking the side of the little guy and outsmarting big-law lawyers for the benefit of the little, less privileged people.

I feel that I am a little bit of both. With Harvey, I share the loneliness, the emotional handicaps, the ability to handle high pressure situations, the solution-based approach. With Mike, I share the passion for the law, caring for the disadvantaged and weak, the sense that you have some talent in life that needs to be put to good use on earth.

Long story short, the show made it seem so cool to be a lawyer. And the thing was, I didn't need to dream about it. I was one already! And I was living in Brickell (the "Manhattan of the South"), had my own firm (even if tiny), and wasn't too bad looking either. I wanted to be like Harvey or Mike. Besides the more superficial aspects and coolness factor, I wanted to enjoy being a lawyer like they did. I was aware of the fictitiousness and how far apart from reality the Suits law life was, but the aspirational goal of cool-happy-lawyering became a sort of goal to me. I wanted to be the best lawyer in the world like they wanted to be. I dreamed of having a big office like Harvey with his name on the door. An office in a big building where the elevator opens straight to the law firm floor with the logo in front. That idea was big in my mind when I designed our new law firm space in Coral Way. Though the building, pre-remodeling, had a wall with a small hallway with a door to the office, I told my architect that I wanted no walls. The entire floor was open, and the doors of the firm are the elevator doors.

As silly as it sounds, Suits changed my approach to my legal career well into my third year as a lawyer or the beginning of my fourth year. It made me want to be the best. I did not care anymore *per se* about immigration, transactions, litigation, or business. I cared about competing in the major leagues. I wanted to be where the best lawyers were, like Harvey, like Mike. I even bought a couple of new suits with a vest and started dressing like Harvey. It was tough though to use a vest in hot and humid Miami, so that didn't last long. I started talking to people more. I started networking the hell out of the firm. Networking wasn't too bad anymore. More confident in myself, rid of the sadness of the separation with my ex, I loved the idea of being single and selling the heck out of my firm. I took care of my body, got fit, bought a new car. I wanted to feel attractive in the dating market, while at the same time not necessarily interested in being taken. It was a good feeling. Feeling perfectly ok to be single, and at the same time sensing some woman around you that would like to take you. A little bit of the Harvey lifestyle. [insert laugh].

The exterior to my newly renovated firm in Coral Way.

A look inside Ayala Law now.

I focused on the firm intensely. And the firm, little by little, started taking me away more and more from immigration into litigation, which, even if I didn't know well, didn't stress me as it used to, or I could handle better because I had more experience. Wanting to play in the major leagues, I discovered class action lawsuits through a friend in Tampa—Felipe Fulgencio. I fell in love with class actions. I started reading books about litigation and class actions. I became passionate about the law, but most importantly about the trade, the art of being a lawyer. I fell deeply in love with the profession, and, at the same time, I became better at it. I started beating other attorneys more often than not.

At this point in my life, I loved being a lawyer and I couldn't be happier with being one. I did not care about dating or anything else. Love was something that required two humans, and in that sense, there was an aspect to it I couldn't control, so I did not stress about it, even as I approached forty. It is not inaccurate to say that Suits took me out of my depression.

But enough of my story. Let's get down to business. Let's answer some questions about what a law firm is, what flavors it comes in, how do you make one, and how do you keep one. I consider myself a student of this business. I've studied and followed hundreds of law firms throughout the years and learned a thing or two about it. I've picked and chosen and designed my firm in my own image and likeness. If you start one, you should do the same.

* * *

CHAPTER 2

HOW TO MAKE A LAW FIRM

2.1. What Is a Small Law Firm?

A business.

At the heart of being successful with a small law firm is a basic understanding of what it is. As obvious as it sounds, I see countless lawyers lacking this basic understanding.

A small law firm is a business. You are not going to succeed with a small law firm if you don't understand, existentially, that a law firm is a business and, from that standpoint, it is no different from a bakery, a restaurant, a clothing store, a convenience store, or any other business for that matter. It is no different, period. I could not emphasize this enough. If you are not persuaded of that, you have a problem, and you should not own a law firm.

In a bakery, nobody walks out with bread without paying for bread. If you go to Publix, there's a guy at the door making sure you paid. At the clothing store, there's a device that beeps if it detects the sensor in your item was not deactivated; and if it was not deactivated, it was probably because you didn't pay for the item. In a bakery or a clothing store, the owner or her employees are going to make sure that you pay full price. Paying half the price is not an option.

This is one of the biggest mistakes I see in law firms; the failure to understand a law firm is a business, and people (clients) must pay before they walk out the door with the product. I am a victim of this lack of understanding myself.

Balance of inputs and outputs.

As the business that it is, a small law firm is nothing but a balance of inputs and outputs. The input is the revenues, the output is the product you sell. What cost you to obtain the product (the output) must be less than what you receive as input—the dollars. This is how you make money.

Clients themselves have a hard time understanding this. "I just have a quick question," "I just need a five-minute call," "I just need to know if I can do X." If you are a lawyer, you've heard these many times. I like to tell my clients, so they understand what they are buying, that "we don't sell potatoes, or tomatoes, that what we sell here is the time we have from 9 a.m. to 6 p.m." We don't sell anything else. We don't sell paper. We don't sell something tangible. We don't sell the time after 6 p.m. We don't sell the time before 9 a.m. We don't sell the time on Saturdays. We don't sell the time on Sundays. Unless you are not on hourly work, of course, which we'll discuss later.[7]

---

[7] Of course, I work regularly before 9 a.m. and beyond 6 p.m. But that time I usually don't sell. I use it to educate myself, write some firm procedure, create some blog post, write some articles for marketing, or write a book about law firms! Things that go more indirectly to the value of the brand. In our bakery example, is like investing in building a new outside seating area, a new

Hence, the time you sell is finite. And when you add your operating costs (X) [what you need to spend to produce the output], the value of your hours must be *hours* (h) times *Dollar amount* (D) is greater than X.

$$(h)\ (\$D) > X.$$

(h)($D) is greater than X by a factor of at a minimum 0.1, but ideally 0.3.[8]

This formula has simple implications. If, for example, in order for *h* (hours) for Y (legal work) to be greater than X (operating cost), *h* has to be $300 and the market is charging $250 for Y, your business model is failing. Something in your systems is making Y cost you $300 and not making you competitive. You have to review your processes and adjust. Likely, you or someone in your team is too slow. Of course, you could have a captive audience that is willing to pay above market value for Y legal work, but that implicates other aspects of the brand that we'll address later.

This basic formula leads us to another basic idea which is that <u>you must be able to quantify time</u>. If you just work casually, don't bill for anything, or are just working on your gut, then that's not a business. That's whatever, a lawyer taking cases, a mom-and-pop shop, but not a real business. A business measures the balance of inputs and outputs. In our day and age, businesses measure and analyze data. Of course, no measurement is perfect, but some level of measurement must exist.

---

canopy, an improved LED sign, etc. Things you don't actually sell but that improve your business and will make you sell more, because now more customers like the idea of seating outside, because your new sign catches more the attention of passer byes, etc.

[8] If you are making over 0.3, then you are one of those that I consider overprized, and that make the legal profession expensive and overall hurts the idea of "access to justice."

At our firm, for example, when we settle cases, our initial offer will always be a number greater than the dollar value of the number of hours spent in the case + cost + a risk factor (on contingency cases). It is the only way I know to determine if cases are profitable. If I know what my hourly rate should be (to make the firm profitable, and be competitive in the market), naturally, the settlement value of a case must be proportional to the hours spent in the case. Of course, in contingency cases other things are at play. And of course, also, not all cases are equal. Some cases turn out to have some negative facts that decrease its value and do not merit you taking it all the way to trial. In these cases, you engage in some type of loss mitigation and sure, you should settle it for less than its otherwise ideal value. Just like the produce store provides a discount for the lettuce that is about to hit its expiration date or that's starting to show black stains. It is the same business principle.

Busy and broke.

Most practitioners do not have a good measuring system and work mainly on their gut. Ours is not perfect either. But at least we try to measure things, and to the extent possible, control the value-income relationship in each of our cases. But even if you are a practitioner who does not generally measure the value of cases, there's one single, simple indicator you will notice and will demand quick action on your part before you rapidly head into bankruptcy and have to start applying for legal jobs—the phenomenon of being *busy and broke.*

I see this phenomenon quite often. If you don't take the time to reflect, take a step back from your business, and the craziness of the practice day in and day out, you will soon find yourself that you are busy and broke. And if you find yourself in this situation, the last thing you should do is get depressed, panic, or make impulsive decisions. This is the time to do an MRI on your business and figure out where the problem is. And it is not very hard to figure the problem if you go back to the basic (h) $(\$D) > X$. In other words, there are only three places you need to look at to figure out why you are busy and broke:

1. Is your hourly rate too low compared to the market?
2. Are your operating expenses too high?
3. Is your output per hour competitive?

I generally find that number 1 is not usually the problem. Most lawyers, based on their years of experience, are pretty good at knowing what hourly rate the market charges.

Number 2 can be a problem. Lawyers get into offices that are too expensive, pay for services they do not need, or pay salaries that they shouldn't be paying.

The most frequent problem I see is item number 3 though. The output per hour is not competitive. Because remember, (h) $(\$D) > X$ does not explicitly factor a per hour of work rate. In other words, can you write an 8-page doble-space motion for a federal case in 8 hours? Or does it take you or your team 24 hours to do so? The reality is 8 pages in 8 hours is what a competitive productivity rate looks like; or somewhere around that number (6 or 7 could be competitive depending on the amount of research involved, or the volume of documents to be reviewed pre-writing).

In other words, productivity is key to the (h) $(\$D) > X$ formula and to be competitive in the legal market. Of course, the 8 pages in 8 hours pace applies only to litigation cases. But transactional cases have their own rate as well. An I-485 (adjustment of status) application package, assuming all data and documents are already in your possession, should not be more than 6 hours of paralegal work. Every type of work has its competitive and non-competitive productivity rate. And this is something that only you as practitioner will be able to know in your respective practice. It is not that difficult to figure out. If you charged $2,000 flat for a non-complex adjustment of status case, you can do the math. How many hours will a paralegal spend on the file, how many hours will the attorney spend on it, add both up and you will come up with a rate per hour for the lawyer and the paralegal. You then multiply that (assuming you only practice immigration) by 40 hours and then by 4.3 (there's 4.3 weeks in a month, not 4), and you are going to get a number. That number is your ceiling, the maximum you could make in a month if you did only adjustment of status cases. Then, go to your bank account, and add all the expenses and see what number is higher. Do it not for one month, but for a 3-month period, and you will easily figure out if you are making money at your $2,000 flat rate, how much money, and what you need to adjust.

Now, productivity rates are not something that is fully human dependent. Not all employees or lawyers can produce at the same rate. Humans' ability to focus vary greatly, with some being able to work for 8 hours straight and others merely two to three hours. Thus, systems will play a factor. Your firm should have systems that improve productivity rates. In brief writing, for example, have specific formats, templates for "legal standards" in motions, and a review process that improves productivity. Your systems can aid the 10-hour brief writer and turn him into a 9-hour or 8-hour brief writer.

This also assumes you and your team have a good work ethic—something that I haven't mentioned because I consider it to be the *sine qua non* of everything. A good work ethic is a prerequisite to everything. Laziness kills businesses.

Find your focus.

A business is a combination of **Product, Experience, Marketing, and Location**. There's really nothing more. As a small firm owner, you will have to decide where you will put your emphasis. Do you want to focus on the quality of your product? Or do you want your clients' experience with your firm to be center? Do you want to be the best at marketing, regardless of the product? Or do you simply pick the best location where clients will simply walk by (like a Regus or WeWork full of professionals in need of lawyers)?

Granted, all firms will do, at different measures, a little bit of each of these four aspects. But the emphasis that you place in one or the other will define your firm as a business. Let's use simple examples. Have you ever gone to a fair or an arena and bought a horrible hotdog but ate it anyways? Well, that's a perfect example of location. The hotdog's quality is secondary. People will buy the damn hotdog no matter what; because it is there, and there's no other hotdog cart to choose from.

If you live in Miami, you must have seen Kendall Toyota dealer advertisings. They are everywhere, and people appear to buy from them; otherwise, the massive advertising budget would not be justified. Is a Toyota in Kendall Toyota really better than a Toyota in another dealer? No. But they market the hell out of their dealer, and because of their emphasis in marketing, they do well.

Publix Super Markets is perhaps a good example of a focus in customer experience. Their stores are clean and organized. Their staff is trained to be nice, everywhere. Managers are reaching out to customers to make sure that, "you found everything you wanted ok?" Compare that to Walmart or other stores where you must beg to pay for what you want, wait in long lines, or rarely find anybody to assist you to find the aisle you need.

Apple and Tesla would be good examples of a focus on the product. They are hyper-focused on product. They are so obsessed with the product that the product then sells on its own, without much effort or a massive marketing infrastructure. In fact, Tesla, for instance, barely does any marketing at all. The product's reputation and quality markets itself.

2.2. What Type of Business Is a Small Law Firm?

A small law firm is what I like to call an anthropomorphic type of business. The business is YOU. The business has or will have your soul, whether you want it or not.[9] If you accept this premise, this should guide everything. If it does, everything will work better. If you understand this premise existentially, then the next logical step is that you have to match the product, the procedures, the methods, and the clientele, to better match your (human) identity, which is the identity of the firm. This of course implies self-knowledge and self-awareness as a condition precedent. Believe it or not, a deep understanding of your psychological profile is helpful. But even if you don't understand your psychological profile in depth, there are simple symptoms of your psychological profile that should inform who you are and in turn, what your firm should be. Think of things you like. There's no better X-ray to who you are than the things you like. The things you like will tell you

---

[9] All businesses are, to a certain extent, anthropomorphic with respect to its founder. But the larger the business, the more its anthropomorphic nature dilutes. Tesla, for example, will outlive Elon Musk. Though I pray it's not the case, Ayala Law, P.A. will likely not outlive Ayala. Most small firms shut down at the end of their leaders' professional life span.

who you are and will, in turn, tell you what to practice and how to shape your firm.

Immigration case in point.

Let me give you an example based on experience. When I started my practice, shortly after being fired from Vernis & Bowling, I had no idea what to practice. Not only did I not have any idea as to what to practice in general, but I didn't know more specifically, what I could sell the market in terms of legal services. In my reflection back then, I thought, I love immigrants, I am an immigrant, therefore, immigration law seems like a good fit. If to that you add that Juan Carlos Gomez was willing to mentor me in the immigration field, as a new solo practitioner with barely 1.5 years of experience, immigration cases seemed like something I could viably obtain. No big corporation will hire a 1.5-year-old lawyer working off his studio in LeJeune to handle their cases. The chase for regular people as clients was more viable.

So, I started my practice as an immigration practice. But soon I realized I was not happy practicing immigration. Back then, the focus of my immigration practice was deportation defense. I didn't know exactly why I didn't like it, but I knew that I did not like to deal with deportation defense.[10] In my view at the time, it would appear I was born to practice immigration. But my view or analysis of the situation was incomplete. Though there were aspects of deportation defense I liked, I failed to see then that there were others for which I was not a good match.

---

[10] Granted, this could have also been affected by my overall dissatisfaction with the legal profession, myself, the career path I had chosen, and my personal and psychological problems. Though I see that in retrospect, I am also able to see how the deportation defense type of practice did not fit me well personality-wise.

Here is how the analysis looks like now:

What is a deportation practice?	Check/No.
Dealing with a complex subject	Check
Helping immigrants	Check
Solid people's skills	No
Dealing with criminals	No

I have always loved, since my philosophy years, complex and intellectually challenging subjects. In that sense, immigration clearly fulfilled that aspect. Immigration is complex. It is vast, diverse, and amorphous. Immigration did not lack the intellectual challenge aspect, and it filled that part of the equation.

I have always loved immigrants and helping them because I am an immigrant myself. Practicing immigration law would literally help immigrants in one of the most direct ways possible. The "helping immigrants" box was clearly checked out.

I have never had people's skills. I am borderline when it comes to emotional intelligence. I've always hated small talk. Immigration required solid people skills and to be compassionate not only internally, but in expression.

I consider myself a compassionate person. But that's not enough, you also have to be able to express properly that compassion, pay attention to people, console them, listen to them, or talk to them for long times. This was clearly not my forte. I simply did not have it in me to talk to people. Solitary in nature, I did not feel comfortable doing that aspect of the job.

I have never liked to deal with criminals. I am a proud immigrant who has had—I believe—a fantastic career in the U.S. whereas in my home country, Peru, I couldn't even find a job. I am extremely thankful to the United States, which is my home for 21 years now, and to all that it has given me. The idea that illegal immigrants, visitors in another's home, engage in rape, domestic violence, drug dealing, theft, fraud, and other crimes—and that I had to defend these—was repugnant to everything I stood for. I was extremely uncomfortable with the idea that—because I needed the money—I had to defend criminal immigrants when I myself wanted them deported. This was perhaps the tie breaker.

What made me realize that this was not a good practice model for me. There are, of course, exceptions. A lot of immigrants in removal proceedings are innocent and are there because of the "crime" of entering illegally. But, at least under the Obama and Biden administrations, these were not a priority and mostly you were dealing with immigrants that had some sort of violation, arrest, charge, or conviction.

But this is me. There are lawyers that are a perfect fit for a full-blown immigration practice. There's this lawyer I follow on Instagram that was simply made for immigration. The guy has a shiny smile on his face, is charismatic, and interacts with immigration clients with closeness, passion, empathy, and love. I simply could not compete with that. I did not have the natural skills to succeed as an immigration lawyer.

A word on capacity – the elephant in the room.

Capacity is, to me, in our profession (specially in law training) the elephant in the room. A business—specially a law firm—requires certain capacity. Not everybody can do this.

Do you have capacity? Do you have the capacity to handle ridiculous amounts of stress without making your life and the life of others miserable? Without running into physical and mental health issues? Do you have what it takes to take on a dozen job duties? Can you be lawyer, manager, HR, IT, lawyer again, negotiator, psychologist, customer service, PR, rainmaker, advocate, financial advisor, lawyer again, scientist, lecturer, teacher, public speaker, lawyer again, all at once?

I don't have an exact definition of the word "capacity," but I chiefly refer to it in terms of mental power. The law requires solid mental power and focus. Law schools are lying to certain applicants. Some applicants are doomed to fail from the moment they enroll in law school.

The tips in this book are worthless to an individual who does not have the mental strength to take on this profession at the most basics of practices.

One lawyer said it best: "There's no yoga-ing yourself out of this." Capacity matters. You cannot be 5'4" and pretend you are going to make it in the NBA. You cannot have X (below what's needed) intellectual talent and pretend you are going to make it in the practice of law. Nobody talks about this, and yet it is perhaps one of the most fundamental things.

If you do have capacity to meet the threshold, then the conversation is what type of practice you should build based on that capacity. Not all practices are equal in terms of stress. Drafting contracts or warnings in labels have nothing to do with a high stakes trial practice where the other side is coming after—not only your client—but you personally. This business can get nasty. It can become an all-out war.

2.3. How to Start a Law Firm Business?

2.3.1. What to sell?

I've told you that a law firm is a business, like the bakery. Therefore, the first thing you need to figure out is: Are you going to sell baguettes, Cuban bread, croissants, rye, sliced bread, pastelitos, muffins, or all of the above?

In your law firm, your practice areas are what you sell. When I started Ayala Law, I started at the beginning of my second year as a lawyer. I knew nothing. I had no cash. I had no connections. I had no mentor. I had to figure out before "who to sell," the "what to sell" question. I didn't even know what I wanted to practice. I had worked for a year at a commercial litigation firm defending big corporations. That line of work had two problems: (1) I didn't like it, and (2) assuming I had learned it in a year (which I didn't), it was not viable as a product to sell. Big corporations don't hire "solos."

2.3.2. How to decide what to sell?

There is no one formula on how to figure out what to sell in your practice. But here are some ideas:

> ➢ **Trial and error:** This is the way I did it. Empirically. The problem with this method is that I wasted years. It is unorganized in nature and not productive. For example, my good friend Eric started his law firm at the same time as me with the single focus of representing businesses. In fact, his firm is called EPGD Business Law. He had a clear idea of what he was going to sell from the start. He did not wander between deportation, visas, contracts, litigation, transactions, real estate, or other areas I've touched. Partially because of his focus—and his talent as a businessman, which I admire—he's built a

fantastic firm and has over 20 attorneys working for him. Being hyper focused on a product, mastering it, will go long ways to developing a successful practice.

> **<u>Vocation</u>**: Some of you simply know that you want to practice and have no doubt about it. Just that puts you ahead of the game. And you don't have to settle for that only, you can later on add other things that are compatible with that one area to the menu. For example, family and estate planning are compatible. Business visas and business law also. Personal injury and tax law? Not so much. At the end of the day, compatibility has to do with client needs. As long as there are clients that need X and Y, the areas will be compatible. Because most business visa clients need a business lawyer, the areas are compatible. Believe it or not, business transactions and business litigation are compatible notwithstanding what you are told in law school about the litigation/transactional duality. There's a dichotomy usually presented that in one world are the transactional lawyers, and in the other the litigators. Business transactions and business litigation, in my humble opinion, go hand in hand. And one makes you better at the other.

> **<u>Opportunity</u>**: You may simply fall on a field based on an income opportunity that is too hard to reject. For example, you may know an adjuster friend that can bring you dozens of first party property damage cases. You may know a chiropractor that can refer to you tons of personal injury cases. If you have the key to the pipeline of leads, it is very hard to reject a particular practice topic in this hyper competitive legal market. Money is always a strong incentive.

> **<u>Where the money is at</u>**: You may like the big bucks (nothing wrong with that). Big money is undoubtedly in big law. If you are well connected enough, if your family has ties to wealth, you may be able, with a small practice, to land one or two big (200 plus employees) corporations and that alone, can make a 3-4 lawyer firm with 4-5 additional support staff. It will be highly profitable billable hours work as long as you can stomach it. Some of us can't handle representing causes we don't believe in or certain big corporations. Some of us are more wired to prosecute cases and to hang with the little ones.

> **<u>Type of paying structure models</u>**: If you have some cash, you may have latitude to choose. You may be able to take on whatever case on contingency until you hit that jackpot that will finance your cases later. Contingency models are fun in terms of not being a slave to the billable hours or having to deal with collection issues. Unlike popular belief, collection issues occur across the board—big law and small law alike. But contingency models can be brutal. A single case can take from 3 to 5 years to go to trial or settle, and, by the time you get a payout, you've done so much work that the payout does not feel as big anymore on a case you've had to finance for so long.

A note on how I decided to practice what I practice today.

Once I matured a little more as a professional—and personally—and having been exposed for a few years to what the real world of the law is, I was able to figure out what was the type of practice that suited me. And the answer came back again to the idea of identity.

A walk through my personality profile is then appropriate here. The <u>first</u> thing you have to know about me is that I have a short attention span; I get bored fast. Because of this, I needed an area that was complex and challenging. <u>Second</u>, I noticed that I was always in love more with the trade than a particular legal topic. I define the trade as the idea of using intellectual skills to gather large amounts of information, organize it, and present something based on it to some adjudicator in an organized and persuasive fashion to further a good cause. In short, I loved *lawyering* more than "property law" or "business law," etc. <u>Third</u>, I wanted to be involved in an area that had a big impact on society. Something where, before I died, I would contribute meaningfully to the world. For example, a case I litigated becoming the source of impactful precedent that positively affected society. <u>Fourth</u>, loving the trade of law and being hyper competitive, I wanted to practice in the major leagues. I did not disdain immigration, I actually loved it, but the world of immigration was not the major leagues. And it is not because immigration is "easy," not at all. The best talent is not necessarily at the hardest of practices. The best talent is where the money is: big law and federal court. To compete with the best, I had to litigate in federal court, and against big law. <u>Fifth</u>, my oral skills were mediocre at best, so, a practice focused more on writing than speaking would be a better suit—without me being an exceptional writer, but in the writing part, with preparation, you had better control. And even though I had limited writing skills, I thought of me as having solid logical and analytical skills. I just needed to learn to put it in words. <u>Sixth</u>, as a natural antisocial, I hated having to interact with people, specially to collect money. The idea of networking was an aberration to me. I was told in law school about the importance of networking, but it never made sense to me. To me, if "I'm good at the law," I should be ok. The years would prove how wrong I was. Networking is everything—unfortunately. You should be afraid of a well-connected lawyer or judge. It matters a lot in our business.

All of these personality traits made me suitable, I thought, for a class action federal practice. Class actions are complex cases, mostly in federal court, that can have a big impact on society. They are all taken on a contingency basis, and the litigation occurs 90% on paper. The competition is brutal, as we are going against the largest firms in the world with the top talent.

While my firm right now handles federal class actions, this is an area that we've developed now for four years, is growing, and where perhaps we are heading more in terms of the percentage of what we practice. Money is an issue in class actions. You just can't take 100 class actions. You need to, little by little, start to build some sort of funds to finance these cases. That's what we are trying to do now. Heading to the future, I would love to have 50% plus of our cases in federal court. Whether consumer class actions, or complex commercial cases. It is not easy to build such a practice, but as a goal, that's what I would like.

My love for immigration though, will always make me take certain amount of immigration cases. To go back to the "how to decide" question, my decision to get into class actions and complex litigation cases, was closely related to better professional self-awareness. The more you know who you are, personally, and professionally, the better your selection of the "what to sell" part of the practice.

2.3.3. Who to sell it to?

Who-to-sell and what-to-sell obviously interconnect, but in my opinion, it's a good idea to have the two boxes separate in your mind, and that you figure out separately what you want to sell, and to whom you want to sell. You could do PI representing consumers or you could do it representing corporations. You could do immigration doing visas for small business owners, South American entrepreneurs whose net worth is $200K, or you could do visas for multinational billion-dollar corporations. To whom you sell what you do matters.

The who-to-sell links also to the type of practice you will have. If you are doing consumer litigation you are going to have one type of practice (contingency), but if you are doing corporate defense work, you are going to have a practice that collects hourly. There's no doubt that you will be richer doing corporate defense unless you become a Lieff Cabraser or one of the large plaintiffs' firms, of which there are very few. In terms of probability, your chances of making millions are higher if you practice corporate defense. That's not to say that you can't do fantastically well as a plaintiff/consumer lawyer. The question you should ask yourself is what will make you happier. Some lawyers don't really care what they do and are able to isolate what they do as a simple "job." I have a good friend who is a partner at one of the largest firms in the world (2,500 plus attorneys). He defends big corporations, and he really doesn't care about the content of his work. He just does what he has to do competently and does not get emotionally involved in terms of consequences of what his work does. His work is just a job. He has the ability—while not being passionate about the law *per se*—to do it at a high level of competence. He does his hours, and then goes home to other things. I find that most people are not like him. Most people tend to find meaning in their work; I certainly do. My work and my practice define me. This is who I am.

But if you leave aside the financial aspect, the who-to-sell relates at the end of the day to who you want to represent, who do you want to benefit with this beautiful tool you have in your hands. You may be the type of person that is unable to represent someone other than the little guy. If that's your case—and you want to build a practice—you must plan carefully.

2.3.4. What type of practice do you want to build?

Once you've done some reflection on the what-to-sell and who-to-sell questions, and have some guidance from the answers, figure out what type of practice you want to build. Let's describe the types of practices that are out there.

Practices are split into two main branches: litigation and transactional. There's no more. You are either litigating or in the middle of a transaction. And litigation is, in a way, a transaction too.

Although the practice of law is stressful *per se*, litigation takes the gold in the stress race. Litigation is deadline intensive and is extremely confrontational. The other side—unlike transactions—wants to kill your case; and you, his. In transactions, both parties have an incentive for a deal to get done or closed. Nobody wins if there's no deal or if the transaction doesn't close. In litigation—though there's mediation and cases settle—there's a huge upside to one side losing. Winning carries not only the highest monetary reward, but pride and honor. It builds your record and reputation. Most lawyers' profiles will include their wins: whether it is an appeal, a verdict, or a bench judgment. It's what we really live for—the W. I call litigation the "emergency room" type of work. In the emergency room, doctors must jump in and act expeditiously to beat the disease or condition. It's stressful, demanding, rushed. I call transactions the "preventive care" type of work. You go to your primary physician without a condition, just for a checkup, to make sure you don't end up—because of lack of checkups—in the emergency room (litigation). At the end of your regular checkup, more often than not, nothing is wrong or there's no emergency to take care of.

In this part I will explain a bunch of practice areas, most of which I have been exposed to, even if by handling a single case. As a small practitioner, you will find yourself sometimes in a situation that you must generate revenue or die. You will find it's not a great idea to say "I only practice X" when someone is willing and able to hire you for case Y. Once you build a clientele, that clientele may not be crazy about some other lawyer handling their legal work, and they may be willing to pay you—even if you have less expertise than others—for a particular legal need. Because of that, I have been exposed to many areas, even if my focus now is civil and commercial litigation.

2.3.5. Are you going to sell litigation?

Within the litigation bucket, there are many sub-buckets.

1) Volume/Contingency/Plaintiff/Consumer Practice.

<u>Personal Injury</u>. Litigation for consumers is mostly done on a contingency basis—you are paid a percentage of whatever you recover. In consumer litigation, you are likely going to be a plaintiff's attorney. Corporations rarely sue consumers (since they are mostly uncollectable) and consumers rarely can afford to pay a lawyer to defend a lawsuit.

In consumer litigation, the most prevalent is certainly the world of personal injury. It is by far the most common area, and where most lawyers end up practicing. The market for personal injury cases is brutal. Billboard after billboard, and referral company after referral company, targeting everyone that walks the earth. It's aggressive. If you can handle that aggressive marketing aspect and the wild competition for cases, then you could do this. Though personal injury is known for being mostly a settlement practice (a lot of cases settle), medium or large firms do not mind taking cases all the way to trial to maximize their value. If you are a lawyer with an interest in trials, this is definitely an area you should consider. Just by the sheer volume of injury cases, the amount that end up in trial is also massive compared to, say, business litigation, which rarely ends up in trial. Also, unlike business disputes or consumer rights disputes, PI cases are not subject to "motions to compel arbitration" or "motions to enforce forum selection clause." In our business, these two are synonymous with winning the case. That is, defense lawyers do not really "want arbitration" or another "forum." When they file these motions, they virtually win the case. You can always sue for an injury in the courthouse of your county. Nobody is going to remove you from there.

<u>FLSA</u> (Fair Labor Standards Act) is another type of consumer/contingency type of practice. These are small value cases related mostly to unpaid overtime by employers. There are three main aspects I believe make this area attractive to practitioners. <u>First</u>, the FLSA statute provides for mandatory attorney's fees for the prevailing party. That's huge. To know that you can prove a single hour of unpaid overtime, and you could potentially recover all your attorney's fees from an "employer," who is generally collectible, is a game changer. <u>Second</u>, the FLSA provides for "liquidated" damages. If you are able to show unpaid OT, your client will be entitled to double the number of unpaid wages. If unpaid wages were $10,000, you are entitled to $20,000 and all of a sudden, the 40% contingency portion of the attorney doubled. Even in cases that settle early, FLSA attorneys will use this liquidation factor as a bargaining tool: "If we go to trial, I'll get double" you will hear in negotiations. <u>Three</u>, the FLSA statute reverses the standard of proof. The plaintiff only needs to plead that X number of hours were unpaid, and then, all of a sudden, it's the employers' burden to prove that these hours were not worked or that they were paid. The FLSA also puts the burden on the employer to keep accurate records of the employee's time. If the employer cannot produce

good records of clock-ins and outs, then the plaintiff is in a good position to win the case. These lawsuits can be a little mean or unfair and there's a lot of bad lawyers out there enticing employees to file these lawsuits. There are also a bunch of frivolous lawsuits where the number of hours is simply made up, with zero backing, which is sad. Small businesses get basically extorted. Given the risk for the employer, and the cost of defending these cases, the employer defendant may settle anyway, making the lawyer a fee.

First Party Property Damage Litigation. Like personal injury, this is also a volume case, consumer practice. These are claims of damages due to hurricanes or other events. The plaintiff is the insured. The defendant is the insurance company. The insurance company will send an adjuster, who will usually value the claim at very low amounts. The attorney, with the threat of a lawsuit, will try to negotiate a higher settlement of the claim, a portion of which, will remain with him as his fee. It is also a practice that heavily settles, and unlike personal injury, it doesn't end up in trial as often.

Of course, there are others, but these three are clearly the main ones.

2) Not Volume/Contingency/Plaintiff/Consumer Practice.

Consumer Class Actions. A class action is, essentially, a group case. Contrary to common belief, you only need a single plaintiff to have a class action complaint. A law firm that practices class action will be faced with an intake describing a pattern of abuse, overcharge, or wrongdoing that affects not only that individual potential plaintiff but many others. Although courts have certified cases with as few as 19 plaintiffs,[11] a solid

---

[11] *See,* e.g., *Tokoshima v. Pep Boys - Manny Moe & Jack,* 2014 U.S. Dist. LEXIS 58769, at *16 n.4 (N.D. Cal. Apr. 28, 2014) (holding that a class of 19 putative plaintiffs satisfied the numerosity requirement of class actions).

class action is usually more than 100 individuals. From a fact pattern, the class action lawyer will be able to tell if the situation affects hundreds, thousands, or millions. The plaintiff's individual claim will usually be too small to be filed on an individual basis. The lawyer will advise the plaintiff, if he is willing to serve as class representative, explain the process, and sign that plaintiff for the class action. Class action cases are usually filed against larger defendants and are defended by "big law" attorneys. The settlement rate of class action cases is even higher than regular cases (99% plus). Unlike non-class action cases, the settlement has to be approved by a judge. Even though class action cases settle, the process from filing the complaint to a hearing on a motion for class certification (which ends up being like a mini trial) can take a couple of years, and it can be quite painful. There'll be intensive motion practice, big fights over the extent of discovery (class certification discovery or merits discovery) and all sorts of motion filing by the big law defense lawyers, including motions to compel arbitration, motions to dismiss, motions for summary judgment, or motions that seek to enforce some sort of class action waiver the consumer allegedly signed. If the big-law-represented defendant manages to derail the case to arbitration, the case is virtually over. In our industry, as I mentioned earlier, a "Motion to Compel Arbitration" is a misnomer for "motion to kill the case." Judges will write an opinion that rationally justifies arbitration and have sentences about "the parties' bargain," the importance of "enforcing contracts," and the like, but it is all a sham. If the defendant wins a motion to compel arbitration, it virtually wins the case. Never, ever, will you see a consumer and his attorney "move to compel arbitration." I could write an entire book about how much of a sham forced arbitration is; perhaps one day.

In class action litigation, a firm could be dedicating one lawyer (or more) full time to work just on the class action. Unlike volume practices, where a lawyer will be handling 100 cases or more, class action will require heavy briefing, and extensive document review and investigation. If it settles, the settlement approval and notice process itself is burdensome and requires plenty of time from the attorney. Paralegals will not be heavily involved other than to coordinate hearings or deadlines. It is quite a different business model than the ones described before.

Some of the most common class actions are securities litigation, products liability, credit reporting, or overtime violations.

<u>Mass Torts</u>. Though related, but not the same, mass torts are also part of this type of practice. A mass tort is, essentially, a class action where the damage is personal injury. Given that personal injury is by definition personal, it is very hard—if not impossible—to get injury cases certified as class action. Thus, this type of mass injury cases is filed mostly as "mass torts." In a mass tort case, you will have 1,000 named plaintiffs, each of whom was injured by the defendant. A typical mass tort is a case where there was some pollution or environmental damage by a defendant resulting in plaintiffs' health being affected *en masse*. In mass torts, there is no "motion for class certification" stage. The cases technically go straight to trial. In most cases though, judges will select a group of "cohort" plaintiffs (15 or 20) who will go to trial first. The expectation being that if the plaintiffs' lawyers are able to win on the first trial group, the defense will have a sense of what's to come and potentially want to settle. Most mass tort cases do not end up trying all of its hundreds or thousands of cases.

<u>Hyper Large Class Actions</u>. There are other types of class actions generally handled by the largest plaintiffs' firms. The class actions mentioned above (like overtime or overcharges to consumers) can also be handled on a

massive scale depending on the defendant, but there are certain types of class actions which are by nature very large and require at least two or three full time attorneys to handle. Privacy would be a good example. If you want to sue Facebook for privacy violations, you are likely going to end up in litigation of a massive scale. Many of these big companies don't settle for two reasons. First, to "send a message." If you want to come after me, they think, you are going to have to spend many millions of dollars in legal fees—which may be negligible to them. Second, big law has a huge incentive to run the case to a certain course. Run the clock, as I like to call it. The big law business requires partners to bring massive amounts of legal fees. A quick settlement will not do it. You'll be surprised how much litigation is lawyer-driven as opposed to client-driven. Therefore, if you want to go against tech giants, your pre-suit investigation, lining up of experts, and yes, very good dependable plaintiffs are a must. That, of course, in addition to a solid budget, one that will get you through trial or the eve of trial. In numbers, you are looking not at thousands but at hundreds of thousands. Securities fraud, price gauging, antitrust, are also class action types that are perhaps not fit for the solo/small practice but for a solid 10-plus lawyer practice. Our firm is unfortunately not there, but I like to think one day we could do this type of work. That's a dream of mine.

3) Medical Malpractice and Catastrophic Injury Practices.

Some practices do personal injury, but they stay away from the regular car accident, herniated disc, type of case. They don't focus on volume, but on cases with massive bodily damage (or death) that will likely present a strong case. These firms can have just 20-30 cases and still make a very decent living with just a handful of attorneys. This type of work usually requires solid intellectual talent since they will be facing great resistance from big insurance and big law. These firms will handle cases like medical malpractice, negligent security, wrongful death, or cases resulting in a complete disability.

4) Small Business Plaintiff Contingency Litigation.

Business litigation—on the plaintiff's side—can also occur on a contingency basis. The problem with contingency business litigation is that it requires a sizeable amount of damages. Generally, in my opinion, to make a business litigation case viable on contingency, you need at least 6 figures in concrete measurable damages. Not the overstated, intangible damages the business owner tells you he has, but damages which are direct and identifiable. If a provider sold defective perishable products to your client and the defective product ruined an entire batch of your client's other perishable items, the ruined items (plus what your client paid for product) are direct, concrete damages that you can fairly hedge on to build your contingency business model. In many business cases, attorneys' fees are a possibility too. However, my advice to readers is to never hedge a case on the hope of obtaining attorney's fees. Value your case—and plan your budget—based on the direct damages out of which you will take a portion, whether it's 30%, 40% or anything in between. Unless it is a towing case under Fla. Stat. § 715.07, an FLSA case, or another case where the statute makes it a must the recovery of attorneys' fees to the prevailing party (as opposed to a "may") *and*, very importantly, the statute does not apply bilaterally (fees against your client), the possibility of fees should not be something that factors greatly in your budget decisions or the decision to take a litigation case. Fee litigation is full of uncertainties and can become, virtually, a case within a case.

In some cases, we've been successful (meaning the case turns out to be profitable) with a mixed contingency-flat fee model in small business litigation cases. Sometimes, we will require the client to pay a monthly fee (anywhere between $1,000-$3,000), pay for expenses (the cost of transcripts, travel, depositions, etc.) and then we obtain a 20% percent of the recovery as opposed to the typical 33% to 40%. The combination of the monthly fee, the coverage of expenses, and the possibility of an additional payout upon prevailing has not turned out too bad for us and has opened the doors of the court to some clients and cases where they would otherwise have been shut, not on the merits of the case, but on the finances.

In general, you must keep in mind that litigating a small case ($100,000 plus in damages) in state court in South Florida will cost you anywhere between $30,000-$50,000; more or less depending on your style of practice, systems, and efficiency levels. So you must budget accordingly. And you cannot get into a case, NEVER, with the idea that it will settle because, while true that most cases settle, from beginning to settlement it could be years. Moreover, if it happens not to settle, and you have not planned, you are going to feel horrible when you have to abandon your struggling practice to focus on this one case that will not pay you enough to cover that. There is no worse feeling in the world than being stressed, overworked, and broke. Budget planning in cases is critical. The client that you will have to turn down will not understand it. They don't fully appreciate the value of your time, your overhead, the cost of your systems. Often, even though you need the income badly to pay for your rent or payroll, you will have to let some cases go, to seek real income.

5) Litigation at Medium Size or Big Law Firms.

I consider "medium size" law firms those of around 20 attorneys. When a law firm has around 20 attorneys or more, it means it has between 50 to 80 total employees. It is really more than a little shop, and the pressure to bring bigger clients (the type more typical of "big law") is great. You cannot run a 50 plus employee business with 3- or 4-thousand-dollar retainers. You'll be routinely asking for $20,000 or more to handle a case. It'll typically be some sort of defense case. Medium size and big law literally have the best business model. You work, you collect. Clients are usually medium to large corporations who can afford a lawyer. Rarely do you see a withdrawal of a large law firm from a case for "irreconcilable differences" (a euphemism for not getting paid). If a large corporation doesn't want to pay its legal fees, it will not go silent on the lawyer and stop paying the bill. It will simply settle the case.

In the big law type of model, you are likely to make good dollars, but you are the least likely to be able to have any say on what cases you work on. The decision to work on a given case is almost exclusively lawyer driven. Partners will have a good, long-standing relationship with large clients, which will guarantee a safe stream of billable dollars. Medium size and big defense firms will recruit the top talent who will use its top brain capacity to derail often times meritorious cases. It is, in my opinion, a business model where the passion for the law is different. I don't know this first-hand, but I've dealt with many big law firms throughout my career. I've seen their big brain associates use their intellectual capacity to take out silly issues out of context in the most intelligent of ways and derail cases on infinite tangents in an effort to exhaust the smaller capacity firms. You will read briefs on silly issues they intelligently make appear as an important issue on procedural grounds or as an "abuse of the discovery rules." I promise you, it's quite incredible. If you have the stomach to do this, and the intellectual capacity to come up with creative ideas and arguments on silly issues, and put them down elegantly in briefs, in a fast turnaround, you will make a lot of money.

2.3.6. Are you going to sell transactions?

Transactions are the "preventive case" type of work. You go to your doctor feeling great to see if everything is ok, even though you are feeling fantastic. And who wants to pay when one is feeling fantastic? Few people. Transactions are like this in many ways. It is the entrepreneur or consumer hiring you to draft a contract when they don't really feel that they need one and actually feel great about the new partnership they just started with this new provider, associate, or partner. In fact, hiring a lawyer to draft something may signal distrust and may "poison" the relationship. What I am trying to say is that, in my experience, in the world of the mosquito law firm, it is tough to make a living writing contracts, or on transactions in general. The product is not as high priced as the work in the "emergency room" and the patient doesn't want to pay—he doesn't see an urgent need to pay for paperwork. I am by no means understating the importance of contract work. I wish more people understood how important a well drafted and negotiated contract is at the inception of a transaction or a business relationship. But human nature gets in the way. And it is difficult for most humans to invest in something when things are going ok.

There are several types of transactional products or practices.

1) Transactional Consumer (At Closing) – Real Estate.

The most typical transaction dealing mostly with consumers—as opposed to businesses—are real estate transactions or "closings," more colloquially. Closings are tricky. This type of work can be messy and complex, but it is for the most part, after doing 10 or 15 of them, routine. The complexity in closings lies not in that it is intellectually challenging (it can be in certain cases), but that in your typical real estate closing, you are dealing with many human beings. And when there are many human beings involved, things get messy. You have a buyer and a seller, two realtors, two banks, underwriters, a broker, appraiser, surveyor, condo association agent, two lawyers, loan processors, title agent, paralegals. Dealing with so many people necessarily creates a complex situation. You'll have these long threads of emails where ten thousand people are cc'd and God forbid, someone's poor email drafting skills put a "tone" (even unintentionally) to the message that instantly creates a chain reaction of responses from someone on the other side that threatens to walk out, and with it, destroy the whole transaction from which 10-plus people's income depends—nobody gets paid if there's no closing. As the closing date nears, things get worse. Emotions run high. Fears of fraud exacerbate. Threats of lawsuits come up.

In the end, 95% of deals close, and people go home. The payout for doing all this coordination work is not high. 2K to 4K on average. The beauty of it though, unlike litigation, is that the case starts on day one, and on day 60 it will be over. It won't drag for years. But in this industry, you can't make a living 2K a piece, especially when the transaction requires so much time. Inevitably, it will be a paralegal driven practice if it is going to be profitable. At our firm, since we don't do this often, we focus on larger deals, 500K and up. The title agent (the firm) makes a commission from the title underwriter that is factored into the price of the policy, which correlates with the purchase price. The higher the price of the property, the more you make. The amount of work is the same, making the higher deals more profitable from the title work standpoint. If you don't have the closing infrastructure to do many closings per month (and streamline the work), being more selective is the option. At our firm, we don't even market this area. We provide the product to our clientele. There are several services we have that are available to someone who is already one of our clients. As a small firm, you will need to have these options. A lot of clients don't want to deal with two or three law firms. They'll want you to do it and to have you—the firm or lawyer they trust—do it, they'll be willing to pay a premium.

3) Business Transactions (At Closing or Up Front or Mixed).

Business transactions—at least what I know about it—involves the purchase and sale of a business. I have never been involved in a large merger or acquisition. All the transactions I've been involved in have been under 4 million dollars in value. Business transactions are like real estate transactions but easier. Replace the real estate for the business. You will usually represent the buyer and act as escrow agent or represent the seller. Rarely is the seller the escrow agent—but it does happen. The work involves all sorts of document drafting and review. Non-competes, non-circumvents, non-disclosures, confidentiality agreements, escrow agreements, purchase/sale agreements, company resolutions, affidavits, assignments of leases, assignments of trademarks, you name it. If you like contract work, this is for you.

There's the other aspect of the transaction though, the one where you have to deal with the humans. Thankfully, there are not as many humans involved as there are in real estate closings, but still, you have to deal with humans that don't trust each other. You, as the attorney for your client, have to strike a balance between protecting your client and not being the deal killer—the insecure overprotective lawyer who drafts un-signable one-sided stuff. There is always a balance to be stricken that has to account for your client's risk tolerance. Some clients will really sign anything, they just want to close. Others will want every single term negotiated and carefully drafted. You must educate them both, the casual carefree one, and the insecure OCD one. This, like most things we do, requires a degree of emotional intelligence and talent to handle humans. The most difficult of which tends to be the opposing attorney.

You can do this type of work by the hour, as a percentage of the price of the transaction, or with a mix flat fee plus percentage. My decision on how to charge in these transactions is on a case-by-case basis. If I see the transaction is safe to close, I may want a straight up percentage fee, specially, if the transaction is high value. A percentage fee could be anywhere between 2%-5%. If I see the transaction is complicated, that conflicts will arise, I will seek an hourly rate with a minimum retainer of 5K to 10K depending on the size of the transaction and the estimate of hours it will take me to do the work. If I have a feeling anywhere in between, I'll ask for a small retainer, to cover my hours in case the transaction fails, and a percentage of the value of the transaction. In any event, unlike litigation, you will be collecting soon. Transactions under 4 million usually don't last more than 90 days.

In business and real estate transactions, you will have to polish your mathematical skills. Closing disclosures can be hard to understand. The way they reconcile can be weird for the social sciences person. At the end of the day, the logic is simple: a bunch of credits and debits in both parties' ledgers that add or subtract depending on the item and that give you a final number for each party. That number does not include—or has already accounted for—certain items that the closing or escrow agent will pay himself: commissions, taxes, recording fees, utility bills, etc.

3) Transactional Consumer (Flat Fee).

When I mean transactions for consumers, I mean transactions for regular human beings.

Immigration Applications. Immigration visa applications are a good example of transactions for consumers. Even immigration litigation is half transaction, half litigation. It will always involve some form filling with supporting documents, an index, and a support letter or memorandum from the lawyer.

Charging in general, but especially in immigration, is an art. You must be careful and charge the correct amount. Immigration cases can last long, and even keeping the file has a small overhead fee. You have to strike a balance between what the client is willing to pay and what the work really costs the way your firm is set up.[12] There will be that breaking-even point where you simply should not take the case. For example, we could charge even $800 for a simple naturalization application where we only do the paperwork, and don't have to appear at the naturalization interview. But a naturalization application with convictions (that you already assessed is potentially approvable)[13] has a different price. We could charge anywhere between 2K to 4K for these cases. I will demand that the client pay for me to attend the interview,

---

[12] You could, of course, make your systems more economical, but that is a macro decision that should not factor in the specific decision of how to charge in each case. When you quote, you better know what your overall cost in that particular practice area is at that moment.

[13] Sadly, in the world of immigration, struggling immigration attorneys or plain mean, greedy ones, will take on cases with an extremely low chance of success. The client—the immigrant—who is looking for a beacon of hope, relishes on the attorney's tone of "approvability," and will pay the fee. This is something that I hope you, my reader, never do. I have a 98% plus success rate in immigration applications. Not because I am special, but because in immigration, unlike litigation, you can tell what a winner application looks like. It's easy to win the case at the intake process.

for example, I would consider it too risky for the client to go alone. The things United States Citizenship and Immigration Services (USCIS) officers do when the immigrant is not represented, especially if the case is a 50/50 proposition, are pretty messed up. In these more complex cases, USCIS may send a burdensome request for evidence (or RFE, in immigration lingo) that will take you hours to respond. A memorandum of law also would be a good idea. It is always a good idea to send USCIS examiners legal memoranda and explain to them why the precedent and manuals support approval of the application. But of course, sometimes budget is limited, and you just can't do it. But in an ideal world, where money is not an issue, you should always send one.

You have to do your research or ask around, so you know what the market charges for these cases. Once you've done a few of these cases, just count your hours and paralegal hours, add them up and fill a four-week bucket with this X hour item. Let me give you a simple numerical example:

Imagine a case takes you, from beginning to end, 16 hours over a one-year period. Now imagine you charged $1,200 for that case. Put these 16 hours in a four-week period.[14] In a four-week period, you have approximately 160 hours of available work capacity. If you were to take just this type of cases (a 16-hour/$1,200 case), you could make a maximum of $12,000 in that four-week period. Your monthly expenses then, have to be less than $12,000. Much less actually, because you cannot think that you will be at full capacity all the time. There will be slow times where you can't bring in 160 hours' worth of work. And if you bring in more than 160 hours' worth of work, you won't be able to take care of it. Let's say your rent is $3,000; your salary $5,000; internet,

---

[14] Most expenses are monthly, so it is not inaccurate to make an estimate based on a four-week period.

phone, and legal software are another $1,000. You are already cutting it close. A business, even a tiny one, has a million expenses. Licenses, E&O insurance, bank fees, gas, parking fees, website fees, social media fees, digital storage, networks, computer costs, employee care, printing fees, membership fees, research software, etc. I mean, it is pretty insane. So, in my hypothetical, you probably must charge more than $1,200 because even though a maximum potential of $12,000 per month may seem ok, it is not.

With time, you will build a sense of it, a second nature kind of instinct about how much you should charge in cases, because like most things we do in this field, there's some science and some art to it. But don't feel bad. Even Walmart or Publix do not have an accurate number of how many apples they sold and how many were lost.

Trademark Applications. I place these ones here because they are different than the "closing" type transactions. Trademark applications, though generally for businesses, are similar to transactions for consumers, at least in the world of a solo/small practice. You are dealing with the individual owner of a small business who wants to register his mark. You fill out a bunch of forms and submit them in the United States Patent and Trademark Office (USPTO) website. The USPTO system can be intimidating, but careful reading—as in everything—will get you through. A USPTO attorney will be assigned to your case, who will make some requests for evidence or recommend certain adjustments to the description of the mark. You discuss it with your client, address the examiner's concerns, and as long as there's no other similar mark in the market, the application will likely get approved. The fees for this vary widely. Most fees vary widely in the legal field. You have the volume trademark filers who will do it for under $1,000 (though God knows what hidden fees they are charging), but if you do it by the hour, this can easily take 5-6 hours of work. By the hour is always the safer bet when it comes to charging for legal work. There's no more accurate measure than that because, like we said at the very beginning of this book, we sell time.

Licensing. Obtaining a license for a client is very similar to obtaining a visa for an immigrant. The work starts by filling out some form. It is followed by a request for more evidence or comments from an examiner. It ends up, hopefully, in an approval. We have done licensing work for clients where we've charged them by the hour at a reduced rate than what we would charge in litigation. I've specifically done two types: AHCA and MSB services.

AHCA is the Agency for Health Care Administration. An "AHCA" license is the license a medical center needs to legally operate at a particular location in Florida to provide medical services. The process is quite like an immigration application. A form, an index with attachments, support letter. You will be assigned an examiner who will make a request for more evidence and comments. Once you've addressed these, an onsite inspection will be scheduled, and after, hopefully, an approval.

MSB stands for Money Services Business. There are various types of MSB licenses (Part I, Part II, etc.) but these are generally the licenses that an entity in the money transmitting business (e.g., Western Union) needs to register for. I've done this work three times for different clients. All three approved. I had never done one before my first one. Same with AHCA. Same with lots of things I've done, to be honest. When it comes to transactions though, whether it is an immigration benefit or a license, save for one or two immigration applications (out of hundreds), our record is probably 99.9% approval. This has not much to do with our expertise or talent but with just doing your due diligence. In this type of transactional work, you can filter an approvable application at the intake stage. If it's not approvable, you can guide the client to develop its business to a level where it will become approvable. Don't be like that greedy immigration lawyer who takes immigrants' hard-earned dollars for a low likelihood of success application.

Liquor Licenses. You could also do liquor licenses. I have never done one, but I would love to. I know a friend who does, works for a large firm, and makes a great living doing them. Like most work with a city or county, it requires connections. Once you are known, this could be a massive money maker.

4) Transactional Consumer/Small Businesses (Hourly, not a Good Business; Hard to Collect).

You can also do contract transactional work by the hour for consumers or small businesses. But remember, this is what I called earlier the "primary care doctor" type of work. Who wants to go to their primary doctor? How many people skip these visits if they are feeling great? This, applied to our industry, means that people don't really want to pay dollars for you to review their contracts. Sometimes, at the inception of transactions—when everything is nice and pretty—they don't even want to put things in writing. But if you find someone that can pay for this work, I find this easy non-stressful type of work that pays the bills. We review contracts, make comments on them, draft opinion letters, and charge hourly, though at reduced rates. But do not underestimate this type of work. You can charge a couple of hours to review a contract, and that's it. After your two hours, you deliver your comments, and the case is over. No years-long nasty, stressful dispute.

5) Transactional Business (Hourly).

The same type of work can be done for bigger corporations. You could charge a big retainer to draft their contracts from scratch and build their manuals or handbooks. If you have the right client, this can be easy, non-stressful work.[15] As good as the money can be on this type of work, I find it the most boring thing ever. But that's me, I've had law clerks and associates that truly enjoy this type of work.

* * *

---

[15] I believe all intellectual work, done at a high level, and under certain time/billing constrains, carries stress. So there's not really a stress-free practice; not even transactions.

CHAPTER 3
HOW TO KEEP A SMALL FIRM

I have sadly witnessed talented attorneys, many from my own law class, open their law firms only to have them close it to go work for a firm. In other cases, they go into real estate sales or other types of businesses, abandoning the field altogether. Of course, some of this may be not due to any deficiency in what they did, but unrelated personal life decisions. But for sure there are many who could have used some business advice. I know some of them to be very talented litigators and thus, unlike me, they had a head start on the "what to sell" part of it.

This is where "how to keep a small firm" comes into play. The "how to keep" is far more important than "how to start." This is where I believe the literature is lacking. You are generally taught "how to start" and "how to manage," but never "how to keep." The "how to manage" question assumes a never-ending flow of business that you just have to "manage." The "how to start" assumes that once you start you just have to "manage." To me "how to keep it" is a whole different question that relates to a combination of branding, marketing, and the maturity of the founder, who is the heart and soul of the business (remember, "anthropomorphic"). I try to explain those below.

3.1. The Product Care and Nurture.

<u>Results</u>. Results tops the list. People like results. People seek a value proposition. You cannot, with some exceptions, have people spend $100 to recover $100. For example, in the world of litigation, a W is only viable about 50% of the time. Even settlement can arguably be considered a loss since both sides are compromising and not getting 100% of what they wanted. Whenever I recommend my clients to accept a settlement in mediations, they always challenge me. The conversation goes something like this:

Me: Based on my experience of doing this for over a decade, I believe $100 is a good settlement, and the value of this case is around that number—at settlement. If we go to trial, we may get $120 or $140, but at what financial and emotional cost to you? It will be time consuming, long, and nasty. If you accept $100 today, you can turn the page, and move on with your business and life.

Client: No, but we have all the evidence. We can win more than $140, we can win punitive damages. They must pay for all the harm they've caused. I've been very stressed over this.

Me: Mr. Client, there's a difference between (a) your damages (the total of what you lost), (b) the damages we can prove with admissible evidence in court, and (c) the damages that the law will decide is the responsibility of the defendant. These three numbers are not the same. I believe $100 is a good settlement, but again, it is up to you. If you want to continue, I am in your team.

Most of the time, I persuade them; obviously, if I believe it's a fair settlement.

But long story short, oftentimes clients do not see settlement as a win, but a loss. Straight up wins in this business—especially if you are in litigation—happens the minority of the time. If you can have a law firm where you win *all the time* then, for sure, you will be a massive success. That, however, would be unrealistic. You have to build a firm knowing that sometimes you will not win. Though you have to try to win more often than not, you have to nurture other aspects like care, trust, and service. If your client knows you left it all in the field, competently, and you still didn't win, he will be happy with you. He will be able to see that the loss was due to factors beyond yours or his control. I've had many clients whose cases I lost come back to me with a new case.

<u>Reputation</u>. Your reputation is everything. People search us all the time in public filings, and I'd like to think what they see is a good, quality product. People also search me personally, especially in social media, and they dig into every single post I make. Although social media requires you to post a lot, and some content will be imperfect, I am always wary of how a given post is reflecting on my personal brand.

Judges also will have a given impression of you/your firm. I believe judges in front of whom I've appeared more than once respect me and my firm's work. This puts you in a great position in a case where the equities are 50/50.

Other attorneys will also develop a view of you. It is not unusual for opposing counsel in a case to refer me a case in an area he does not practice. Because even he has a high regard for our work. I was once litigating an extremely contentious commercial case. And during the case, I get a referral for a potential case. When I asked the lead how he heard from us, he gave the name of the opposing counsel in that contentious commercial case. At the time, I did not have a great relationship with that opposing attorney, but he still thought of me because he thought our work was competent. Later, after the case was over, we became friends. I recently settled a case involving a two-million-dollar fraud. Afterwards, the opposing attorney, a very competent 65-year-old practitioner called me to thank me for my professionalism and to say he enjoyed working with me. My colleagues' view of me is very important to me personally in that it also matters to business.

Quality Control. You have to have some sort of way to control the quality of your product. This is the part where your team may hate you a little bit. But you have to control that the output is not only acceptable in rate but in quality. Although the relationship with the client is very important in our business, the quality of the product has big implications in terms of your reputation in the industry and the results you may obtain. We are in a business where the product is words and ideas. The way you express words and ideas matters and has a huge impact in your credibility. Sloppy work makes you less credible.

3.2. Marketing.

I don't believe you can build a serious business without marketing. I've learned this the hard way. You have to be willing to spend a decent chunk of your dollars in marketing. I believe that chunk should be somewhere around 20% of your budget, give or take, depending on the type of practice. Marketing will bring you not only new leads for cases, but it will develop your brand. To a certain extent, it will make your firm less anthropomorphic. While, in my opinion, it is virtually impossible to take a small firm out of its anthropomorphic nature, you should—paradoxically—strive to do that constantly. You should strive to build a brand, even if that brand is ontologically linked to your persona. To do this, you have to be patient. You will have to spend much needed dollars in marketing that will not be directly linked to leads for cases. You have to play the long game.

3.2.1. The clientele database care and build up.

Your clientele is everything. People go to the same barber for years and don't change. They do so more to the same lawyer. Trust is everything. People will trade quality for trust. And if you are able to develop a strong relationship of trust with your clientele, they will be extremely loyal to you, just like they are to that barber who always gets their haircut the way they like it. I've seen amazing clients (high net worth, good paying) trust extremely incompetent attorneys and take their horrible, incompetent legal recommendations. Trust works wonders.

Now, you are inevitably going to lose some of your clients. Nobody has a 100% retention rate. Especially with so many lawyers out there. So, you need to figure out your retention rate, replace the ones you lost, and find more so you can grow. When you hear that saying that you are either growing or dying in a business, this is what it means. It means you are "growing," because if you are not (i.e., replacing the loss in your book of business), you will disappear.

And in our business, a business where we sell such an intangible service, connection is key. Keep in mind that more often than not, the client does not really understand what we are doing for them. More often than not, they have to trust you. And you only develop a trust relationship with personal contact and interaction. I continually network with my own clients. I frequently go to lunch or for drinks with them. If I haven't seen one for 4 or 6 months, I shoot them a text and try to reconnect.

"*A Note on Networking*"

I've learned the importance of networking—and to network—the hard way. I remember that in law school, or at the beginning of my career, I hated networking to no end. I am an introvert, anti-social, border line misanthrope. It is fair to say that I have changed a lot during my business career. Business has, literally, changed me. It didn't make sense to me to "network." I had a simplistic view: "If I do good work, clients will come. I don't need to talk to people for cases to come."

To say I was wrong is a massive understatement. <u>Networking is everything</u>.

But let's define what networking is. Google's definition, which comes from "Oxford Languages," says that networking is "the action or process of interacting with others to exchange information and develop professional or social contacts." That's not a bad definition.

Now, have you found yourself at a big networking event, grudgingly meeting two or three people, pass a couple of business cards to then think: what a big waste of my time! These three people I met have nothing to do with what I do; they'll never send me a client.

If you've found yourself in this situation, you are not alone. A lot of people find themselves in this situation, and understandably so. Unless you are one of those so-called social butterflies, you may get frustrated by the idea of "networking."

But here is the key. Networking is a long game. Rarely will you find a case at a networking event. You have to be willing to "waste" some time, in order to find cases.

Now, it doesn't have to be exactly like that. It can also be more surgical. Here are two things that I've done that have really changed my view and experience of networking, which make it actually enjoyable.

First, like I mentioned, be more surgical about networking. You have to network with like-kind professionals. For example, if you are running a 10-attorney law firm that takes on corporate cases, it makes no sense for you to network with a 21-year-old realtor that just got his license (no offense to realtors). The realtor will provide no business to you, nor will he have a network he can transfer to you. Your network, while maybe useful to him, will also be unlikely to work with such a young inexperienced agent. There has to be somewhat of a match between the individuals networking. I like to compare this to tennis, my favorite sport. I play tennis at a 4.5 level in the tennis level system. I can play with a 4.0 and have a decent time. I can play with a 5.0 and have so much fun. But if I play with a 3.5, it will be boring. If I play with a 5.5 it will be frustrating because I won't be able to compete. Efficient networking has some similarities to this parity in tennis. Go 4.0 or 5.0. Don't go 3.5 or 5.5, it's not going to be productive or enjoyable.

Second. Learn to really connect *and* care. This has been a little bit of a life changing thing for me. I learned that the best way to network is to create a real connection, and to not worry about business at all. I go to lunch meeting and events, and I really want to learn about that person, their life story, their families, what they like, and their interests. I then find similarities between their interests and mine, and we connect. This way, we establish deep connections that last. This connection keeps me in their minds and vice versa and, when a case comes around, they think of me and vice versa. This connection also makes them trust me a lot, which is key to obtaining cases. This is really what networking should be. If you go network with a pure, naked business/money appetite, the person you want to connect with will see it—even if unconsciously—and you won't ever connect. You may get a case here and there. But where business really happens (long lasting business) is when you connect at the deeper, human level.

When it comes to the legal field, it is a no brainer that networking with lawyers is key. Normal people don't have a well-defined concept of specialization. People generally think of specialization (with exceptions) at the "profession level." In other words, they think about doctors, accountants, lawyers, architects, engineers, etc. They don't think of PI lawyer, tax lawyer, immigration lawyer, etc. The average person, when they have a legal need, will contact the one lawyer they know, or the lawyer brother of the friend they know. They won't think, wait, I have a PI issue, does the brother lawyer of my friend practice PI? No. People think that lawyers know laws.

This general assumption in the marketplace makes key networking with lawyers. Lawyers will get leads of all kinds. The maritime lawyer will get a lead for a property claim case. The tax lawyer will get a lead for an immigration case. The immigration lawyer will get a lead for an employment rights case, etc. It is key you are connected to other lawyers—specially your former classmates, since they will trust you, assuming you seemed trustworthy in law school—because they are a constant magnet for leads for cases.

Now, what I said about surgical, smart networking, does not mean that you don't network in other ways. As a businessman, I am networking

24/7. Business comes from all sources. I like to say that cases come from under the table; from where you least expect it. As long as you are talking to some human being, you'll be in business.

Though not my first go-to option, if you are one that is very sociable, large events could be a great source of networking. Judge receptions, fundraisers, celebrations, etc. They are good, even if you don't actually get cases. Some networking could target intangibles in your practice. For example, if you practice in Miami-Dade County, wouldn't it be nice to go to a Miami-Dade County Bar gala where all the Miami-Dade County judges—many of whom you appear in front of—will be? Of course, it would. In our business, if your practice litigation, relationships with judges matter.

3.2.2. Brand marketing.

Whether you want it or not, you have a brand. And that brand has to be promoted. Brand marketing is very important. I have not read any books about branding, or marketing for that matter, so I am not sure if my understanding of "brand marketing" is appropriate from the point of a marketing professional. But still, let me tell you what I understand as "brand marketing."

Brand marketing is the type of marketing that does not necessarily target leads, but that cements your image out there. For us, brand marketing is key for the leads we generate through other means. Once we obtain a lead, and have the initial contact, the lead will go online and search the heck out of us. Given our presence online (which I like to think it's good), they will come back to hire us more often than not.

What do you do to market your brand? You advertise online. Everything happens online. Unless you are Morgan & Morgan, you will not use TV.

What do you advertise? We advertise or show the public through organic content five things: firm news, firm results, firm publications, the people at the firm (mainly me), and firm events. Lately, it's been more focused on me. It's hard to demand my team to create content. I have—the hard way—come to understand that it is important for me to be a personality out there in order to grow the brand and the firm. It's just inevitable. I hate being on video, but there's no growing the Ayala brand if Ayala is not out there; it's simply impossible. We go back to the very beginning of this book; this is an anthropomorphic type of business. Your image as a firm leader is key. People want to know your life, reputation, results, your intellectual reputation. For a couple of years now, we've put emphasis on this.

<u>Publications</u>. It's hard to get published, but people respect those who are. It is important every now and then that me or someone at the firm gets published. Not only does it market competence, but in today's hyperlink hyperconnected online world, these article links within your site will improve your organic reach.[16]

Individual accolades are important, unfortunately, for marketing. Some entities like Super Lawyers (of which I am not a fan) have built large directories that are very visible online. You want to be in these lists. They will improve your searchability. Although there's really no connection between the competence of a lawyer and his "super lawyer" status, being in the Super Lawyer directory is a good thing for marketing. I know highly incompetent lawyers who are in Super Lawyers. The best lawyers I know, are not there.

---

[16] Organic reach means the reach you have through unpaid content as opposed to paid advertising.

Being featured in news articles or magazines of high impact is also important. Specially periodicals that are read by lawyers like the Daily Business Review or Law360. Since lawyers are the best source of referrals, being where lawyers read matters for marketing.

Featuring your personal life matters too. You family, your hobbies. Your prospects want to see the real human. If you want to be in business, forget about privacy. All of this matters to the consumer. They add credibility to the product you sell. In a world full of internet scams, consumers will trust they have a family life lawyer, or in my case, a lawyer who seems like a decent man. They will trust that this profile they saw will not scam them.

3.2.3. Defining your brand.

It is important that you define your brand conceptually. That you are clear as to what defines your brand. I have at the front of my website a "Why Ayala" section that is intended to do just that. The little statement is meant to encapsulate who we are as a firm, and why a customer should select us.

When defining the brand, you must be aware of the type of firms that are out there. The world of law firms is divided in a series of dichotomies as follows. Of course, with some overlap.

1. The plaintiff _versus_ defense law firms.
2. The consumer rights _versus_ corporate law firms. (Little guy versus powerful guy idea).
3. Large, small number of cases (quality) _versus_ volume practice (quantity, low price).
4. Litigation _versus_ transactional.

5. Highly specialized (tax, criminal, social security, maritime)[17] _versus_ full service, "one-stop-shop" idea. (For consumers or businesses).

6. Highly specialized (antitrust, ERISA, tax) _versus_ full service. (For businesses).

What firm do you want to be? In which dichotomy bracket will you fit? And in which side of the bracket? You will need to have some sort of emphasis. Doing it all does not necessarily mean no brand, but that your brand is the "one-stop-shop" type. Customers like that too. We, for example, do a bunch of things not listed in our practice areas for our long-term clientele. I like to think we fit in the left side of the first three brackets. Overall, we know that we target quality. We know that our brand is connected to high quality and deep care for our clients—consumers, immigrants, small business owners. "We don't sell Toyotas," I like to say. We sell Mercedes-Benzs. We also don't sell Lamborghinis or Ferraris (big law?), those are overpriced and overrated.

You may not fit in a single bracket; ideally you should, but if you can't (like I can't), know that they exist and clearly understand your focus. Every single piece of content I put online, has these in the back of my mind.

Be careful of stigma.

If you are about to start your law firm, be careful with what practice area you choose. The practice area you market first, will stick in the market for a very long time. When I first started my practice, I started it as an

---

[17] These are just some examples that come to mind. Lawyers in these areas usually do not have large volume practices.

immigration law firm. Ten years later, people still think that I run an immigration practice and that I am only an immigration lawyer. The reality is that now only 20% of our work is immigration and 80% of it is litigation. What I am trying to say is that if you are not sure you will be practicing topic X forever, be careful how you portray your firm, especially when you are starting. Ideally, I agree with the idea of specialization. One or two topics at most. And mind you, I am giving you advice that is contradicted by my own behavior (we are not perfect by any stretch). We practice 3 or 4 areas of law. But at the end of the day, it is easier to promote a "personal injury firm," "employment law firm," or "criminal law firm." It's still viable to promote an "immigration and family law firm" or "injury and property claims law firm." But promoting an "immigration, litigation, consumer rights, and real estate law firm," is much harder. But personality-wise, I have not been able to settle for a two or one topic law firm. It just becomes too boring for me. This goes back again to the anthropomorphic nature of the firm. This is why our emphasis is not the subject matter but the values: quality, honesty, competence, care. We constantly tell our clients: we will not make you spend $100 to recover $100; a lot of firms—believe it or not—will do that, especially in big law. I have seen big corporations spend a million dollars in legal fees against us only to then settle the case 3 years later for $150K, the same amount we asked on day one of the lawsuit. Who is one million dollars richer? The law firms.

At the end of the day, the ultimate question, the answer to which will determine whether you are going to remain in business is *value.* That is the most powerful brand. It is a no brainer. If you are not adding real value in people's lives, businesses, or society, you may start a business, but it will not last long term (unless you are constantly taking new clients and losing them; a Ponzi scheme?). Nobody has a 100%

retention rate. But your retention rate should be at 80% plus. People are by nature loyal to the lawyer. So you have a head start on that point. If you are losing more than 80%, you have a problem.

I think we are at 90% plus. One of the problems we've had is we've lost our immigration clients because our infrastructure couldn't keep them. Another factor is that it is an extremely competitive market out there. Every year, hundreds of new lawyers open their practices, and when they open, they have the luxury to charge rates you can't now. This underscores the importance of keeping your firm model lean. If you add real value though, you will keep your clients.

Case in Point

Let me give you one example of how our firm adds real value to cases. We had a case where a guy scammed our client into investments that never happened. It is not infrequently that scammers will abuse the bankruptcy process, and file a phony bankruptcy claim with the hope that you will give up in the civil case. At worst, the bankruptcy claim will delay the case for about 6 months or more, and at best, you will give up. Most of these scammers though, will not qualify for a bankruptcy discharge. What do we do? In at least two occasions that I can recall, we've chased them down in the bankruptcy claim. Not by simply filing a claim as one of the creditors, but by filing an adversary proceeding in bankruptcy court. An adversary proceeding is, essentially, a lawsuit in bankruptcy court. Bankruptcy law and procedure are extremely complex. But we love complexity. Our team was able to figure out the process, and the pressure our adversary proceeding put on the phony debtor got the bankruptcy case dismissed faster. As part of that learning experience, me and my right-hand, Luis F. Quesada, Esq. wrote an article that was published by the Florida Bar Journal.

You can find this article here:

https://www.floridabar.org/the-florida-bar-journal/understanding-unliquidated-securities-claims-under-%C2%A7523a19-in-chapter-7-cases/.

Now, this is not how it works though. In a "normal" law firm, the law firm will ask the client to obtain bankruptcy co-counsel with expertise in these adversary proceedings. An additional fee that clients, more likely than not, can't afford and makes the case not viable. This is what I mean by the idea of "value." Our ability to handle complex matters, the talent to learn things fast in areas priorly unexplored, makes us more agile, lean, and valuable to our clients' cases. The same applies to appeals. "Normal law firm" will request appellate counsel when cases need to be appealed. We are great briefers and are able to handle our own appeals in virtually any court, state or federal.

3.3. Other Items That Will Help You Keep Your Firm.

Limiting personal spending and a salary.

Don't be cheap, but limit spending. One of the things that has helped me here is to use a single operating account. This makes things very simple. The account goes up and down. And when it goes down to the bottom, you know that you got to do something about it. You know that you must bring in new cases. If it goes down to the bottom frequently, and you are signing cases, then you know that you must cut on expenses or charge more.

But perhaps my very first advice, since this book targets small practitioners and small firms, is that you control your own personal expenses. I live on my firm's salary. It's been eight plus years that the firm has been paying me a salary. Every payroll I am financially disciplined enough to pay me a salary (because remember, if cash flow is slow, you could choose not to pay yourself, so you can make payroll). But I find that paying yourself is extremely important for separation of person and business. I have a good CPA who has educated me on this and has kept me disciplined about it. I tend to live a frugal lifestyle, so my salary has always been enough to cover my personal expenses. I have this philosophy that my salary will never be more than the highest paid person at the firm. Ten years later, it is still the case.

I've found that learning to live on a salary, like an employee does, helps you keep your business finances healthy. A lot of problems small businesses run into financially is that the owner drains the company and overspends himself. So, try to live on a salary and don't ever skip paying yourself. You will get used to it, just like the electric bill that you cannot not pay because power will go off, so should be your salary. Put it in your brain, "I cannot not pay me," and the brain works wonders.

Profits.

All of the firm profits, I reinvest in one of two: the firm, or real estate. I don't have the exact figure, but I'd say is something around 70/30 (firm/real estate). But then, my real estate investment profits all go to the firm too. I don't take from the real estate cash flow for myself. It all goes to the firm. I have this problem that I love the firm so much I don't mind investing all my money into it. The firm provides me with identity and a reason to wake up every morning. That's the firm you should try to build. A custom-made law firm where you want to reinvest. Don't spend profits in Monaco at the casino. You never know if you'll have these kinds of profits again. In my specific case, I've made some poor decisions in case selection. I've sued big corporations and some of these cases have become a mess. The firm has had to finance them. I feel it is only fair that I finance the firm as well. My team shouldn't pay the price of my poor case selection decision making. In my mind, until each member in my team earns a salary I am satisfied with (I am not there yet at all), I will keep reinvesting every dollar the firm makes (and every dollar of from the real estate business), in the firm.

Another point is not to go on a hiring spree if your firm experiences additional cash flow or profits or it's busier than usual. Remember, if you have eight employees, and you hire two more, now your payroll is for ten people forever. Before you had to feed eight, now you have to feed ten—forever. Of course, if you are one of those that don't care about firing people, then it should not be a problem to you. But if you care—like I do—then by hiring more people, you are putting a big responsibility on your shoulders. You now have to feed a bigger family. That is unfortunately how I see things.

I believe you should only fire based on incompetence. If there's no business to feed your ten, you go seek the business and hustle; you don't cut personnel. Each of your employees depends on the salary you pay them to pay their bills and care for their families. They may have planned a family vacation for which they spent a lot of money, and they expect to have that job when they get back from it. To me, these things should be a factor in the decision to downsize when business is slow.

Technology.

You will not survive in today's business world without technology. Forget the "I am not a techie person." In today's world, especially the world of business, to pretend that you will get away with not being tech savvy is naïve/ridiculous. You might as well not be in business at all, and work for someone else. It's kind of like saying, "Oh, I'm not a cellphone person," I like landlines. To pretend that you will survive in today's world without a cellphone is ludicrous. I am not telling you to learn C++, or Java, or photolithography. I am merely asking you to learn to use what these computer geniuses' incredible hard work has already created! Just use their stuff!

Automate as much as possible without affecting personal contact with your clients, or becoming a form-based, factory type law firm. In a hypercompetitive legal market, consumers crave personal contact more than ever. It makes a difference. Generally, potential clients will go to the personal, sensible, incompetent lawyer before they go to the competent, but cold, distant lawyer. While you should automate, have channels for people to talk to someone in your team.

Calendar.

Regardless of the practice type you have, you need a calendar. Believe it or not, a firm that masters a calendar has an edge over practitioners that don't. This may seem like an exaggeration, but it is not. I don't believe I can count the number of times I've seen lawyers miss deadlines.

Calendaring may seem simple, but it can get tricky. There are, of course, a number of calendaring options out there. But the problem does not end there. Even when you've found the perfect system to use (Google, Apple, Clio, Outlook, etc.), you still need a system in place to make sure data entry is precise. You also need a well-trained team that knows what goes where and how to count dates. For example, if you run a litigation practice, your calendar system is worthless if you don't have a person who knows how to count days for purposes of calendaring deadlines.

The event won't calendar itself. Someone human has to read a paper that came via the court's e-filing system and figure out what the deadline to respond to that paper is. Someone in your team has to understand procedure to know that, in certain cases, a reply is needed, and in others, not. This then must be coupled with a good task system where a task is created to execute on that deadline. The calendar entry is of no use if no one is assigned to take care of it.

As I said earlier, and I emphasize again, a good calendaring system will give you an edge over 50% of other law firms. Large firms (or "big law") rarely miss deadlines (even though they do at times). But generally, when I litigate against large firms, my experience is that they are extremely on top of deadlines. It is the little firms, the solos, whom I've seen missing deadlines—or even hearings—more often.

Make your calendar human-centric as opposed to event-centric. What I mean is that if there's an event under my calendar for example, it means I am not going to be available at that given time. This, as opposed to making a "hearing calendar," let's say, where the entry is not linked to any individual's calendar. I feel that human-centric calendaring works better.

In terms of what calendar to use, I recommend Google. At my firm, we've been using it for a while and find it very convenient. It links to our email, to Google Maps, to our management software, to our phones, etc.

In my firm, the calendar is everything. It's the heart and soul of the firm. When we do our weekly case-review meetings, the first thing we do is go over upcoming events in the calendar, and make sure they are well taken care of.

Management software.

A main billing and case management software is key. I've tried a few in the past and I've also been without one (just a spreadsheet). In the end, I settled for Rocket Matter. We've been using it for 6 plus years now. There are several things I love about Rocket Matter. First, it is very user friendly. It's like the Facebook of case management. It has a stream for posts, tasks, and other user-friendly functionalities. It links to our Dropbox filing system and to Google Calendar. We don't use all of its functions. The main ones we use are the note taking, case organizing, contacts option (to keep a database), and the billing option (to track our time and issue invoices).

Though I prefer Rocket Matter, I dare say all case management software is about the same. None is going to be a make it or break it factor. Just like Lexis and Westlaw are about the same. They'll all give you the case you want. Do use one though, they will keep you more organized.

Website.

The ABA Legal Technology Resource Center did a study on how consumers choose a lawyer and they found that 19% of people decide on a lawyer based on them having "a great looking website." Think about that. You have a presentable website (your product may suck) and just because of that you get a head start with 19% of the potential universe of buyers.

I see lawyers with unpresentable, embarrassing websites. Websites that you can tell have not been touched since the day the guy launched his firm. The impression it gives is terrible. We at our firm make sure we are always putting something new in our site, so people get the feeling we are active, moving, upgrading. We make sure our website looks professional, that the overall impression is of a group of professionals doing competent work. It is hard—or perhaps impossible—to convey trust through a website. That's something that you develop in other ways. It is possible to convey professionalism via a website. And professionalism is sort of the entrance to the trust house. If you look professional, they may call you, and after talking to you or someone in your team, they'll start to trust you.

I am not an expert at Search Engine Optimization (SEO), but you want to work with someone that knows it and keeps good metrics. You want for example a decent bounce rate. A "bounce rate" is the rate that measures the ratio between those who click on your website and read, and those who just "bounce" out. To keep a good bounce rate (somewhere higher than 20%), content is key. The more quality content in your website, the better your bounce rate will be.

3.4. Team Building – Employees.

If you can't build a team, you'll forever be a "solo." Or a "solo" and a secretary. Team building is key to keep a firm. Otherwise, you'll forever be doing everything, including things that as you age professionally are not economically clever for you to do. When you have 15+ years as an attorney, your knowledge is so valuable, you should spend your time strictly on two things: practicing law and client relations. You should be the best at these two; better than anyone at the firm.

I have my own hiring and managing philosophy. I did not learn it anywhere. I believe my managing style is simply a reflection of my personality (anthropomorphic, again).

I govern my firm with a "let them do whatever they want" philosophy. Of course, with some limits, but as a matter of company policy, I literally say: "don't do the things you don't like." You don't like hearings, write. You don't like writing, go to hearings. You don't like talking to people on the phone, email. You don't like email, call them. You are not a people's person, be a clerk. You are not organized, do customer service.

I believe that people gravitate towards whatever they gravitate. And forcing them into something they don't gravitate to, is unnatural, and does not work in the long run. At a company, employees generally seek stability, long term security, and comfort. They all expect that, at the end of the day, "work is work" and therefore, it will never be conformable. But to the extent possible they can feel comfortable, secured, understood at their place of work, and they'll stay long term.

My philosophy is also aligned with Warren Buffett's "we don't hire 400 batters to teach them how to bat." Or Steve Jobs' "we hire smart people for them to tell us what to do." In my firm, because of what we do—complex litigation—we need talent. And I don't believe in telling talent what to do. Often, the talent in my team knows better than myself. I finetune decisions or arguments here and there based on experience. But for the most part, I don't question the product they bring to me. In fact, when we have a new hire, and I have to tell them what to do, what to argue, what to write, it usually is a person that does not fit well in the team. All I do as firm leader is to establish certain parameters (in form and substance) as to what our litigation philosophy is. This philosophy can be expressed in things as simple as "we don't make bullshit arguments," or "we don't file bullshit (frivolous) cases," "we file perfect papers, typo free," "we provide solid logic in papers," etc.

Of course, we also have more specific writing guidelines. I believe uniformity—in form—is key when you are trying to build a brand.

I also believe micromanaging is overrated. If you have to micromanage someone, they probably shouldn't be in the firm. There are so many overhead costs associated with micromanaging.

Also, don't bother them on the weekend. Work is stressful. Specially if you have the pressure to keep a certain productivity rate. Humans don't feel the same every day. Employees come to work on a given day and they may have had insomnia the day before. They may have broken up with a boyfriend (or just had a bad fight) and feel depressed. They may have a headache, feel nauseous, etc. They are there with you, but they don't necessarily have the physical, mental, or psychological capacity to deal with the pressures of the day in optimal fashion. That's why you need to respect their weekends. In fact, at the firm, we have a 39 hrs. per week business model, and we rarely stay overtime. What this does— in my opinion—is give them mental relief. They know that though they have to do X, Y, and Z from 9:00 a.m. to 5:00 p.m., (and X, Y, and Z are stressful), they also know that after 5:00 p.m. it's over and they can go home, watch Netflix, dinner, be with their kids, etc. They also know that on Fridays (after 4:30 p.m. in our case), they'll have two full days where they don't have to think about anything work related. In my opinion, that provides psychological relief, and helps with stress. Quit the silliness of crazy hours and focus on productivity. 99% of the time, what can be done in 10 hours, can be done in 8 hours.

Be aware of the employee curve.

There's such a thing as an employee curve. I am sure someone out there has written about this. All employees start amazing, with rocket speed, high quality, and massive productivity. They all don't stay at that level, and you have to learn to manage the curve. You have to make sure they keep at a pace where the input and output balances push the firm forward. You can't do this if you don't measure things. (*See* 2.1. *supra.*). The idea is for them, overall, to keep a mean productivity level that's optimal to the firm's profitability. We know, for example, writers at the firm have to write between 6 to 8 pages of quality briefing per day. Less than that and it's not profitable. Productivity measuring is not an exact science, but with time, you will get good at it. I sense it. I know when productivity is not there, and when I do, I give them hints, I push them a little bit so they can go back to that optimal level I know they can achieve. Ideally, you want employees who, when they start, show you that they can reach an amazing level of productivity; that way you know that, when things settle, that employee will be able to keep a good average that does not fall below that mean productivity needed for the firm to be profitable.

* * *

CHAPTER 4
EXTRA CREDITS

There are several other items that are important to be aware of and that have helped me build and keep a firm. They are mostly loose items from notes I took to write this book and for a presentation I made once about how to build a law firm. I thought important to share these, even if they didn't fit in a particular section of my outline for this book.

FOCUS! FOCUS! FOCUS!

I believe we currently live in a "focus crisis." Discursive thought is being challenged by a million sources of distraction, mainly via social media. The competition for content views incentivizes the creation of very short, catchy videos or articles, so you can get that "view." Novel reading, book reading, long plot watching are the exception rather than the rule. Deep, hyper focused activity has been segregated for those who create the very sources of our distractions: computer scientists.

But you can't achieve anything meaningful in life if you don't focus. Quite the opposite; if you visualize and focus, you can do anything. This is backed, time after time, by neuroscience research.

I am particularly naturally un-focused. I have an attention problem. I've been aware of it for a long time. But my passion for intellectual work was bigger than my focus deficiencies. Therefore, I use methods or environments where I can counter that deficiency, because, again, if you can't focus, you can't do anything meaningful in life or business.

This is how I do it:

> I have 3 hours that I call "concentration time."[18] If anyone bothers me or knocks on my door from 7:00 to 10:00 a.m., it better be that someone was murdered in the firm's elevator. If you don't block times to do certain work, you'll get nothing done. In fact, this book was prepared during these sacred portions of my day. After these three hours of what I call "deep work," my mind is not the same or as efficient at "deep work" anyway. I move on to other tasks. I open my door because your team needs to bother you. They need to ask you questions, and you need to apportion time to be bothered. Otherwise, things don't get done or the firm does not run in the direction you need it to run.

> I make a list of tasks, and I apportion time to them. When I start doing them, I put headphones on, music, and I set up a timer. This habit is so ingrained in me, that once I put the headphones on and set the timer, I am a hyper focused machine, at least for that short period.

> Social media is important, but it distracts you. I have "Facebook" or social media times too. On my way to work,

---

[18] I don't get 3 hours every day, because sometimes I have hearings at 8:30 or 9:00 a.m. I am generally at the office between 6:30 and 6:45 a.m. And I start working no later than 7:00 a.m.

around 11:30 a.m. (lunch time), and then after 6:00 p.m. I also may check it out during the day in-between tasks.

> You have to learn to say no to people. People like to talk. People like to hear themselves. Cut them down. The day flies by. Unless it is networking, where you literally need to do a lot of small talk (which I hate), avoid unnecessary calls. Text and minimize meetings. The "hey, how are you? how was your weekend?" stuff can take 3 minutes. Five of those calls, and 15 minutes of your life are gone. That's .3 that you didn't bill or collect. I am not anti-relationship, not at all. Relationships are important for business and for happiness, but when it comes to business-operations-logistics, keep it short. There is no time!

COMPASSION AND CARE

Compassion and care work wonders when dealing with your clients.

For example, I have not been able to win (or collect) in all my cases. What works the most in these situations is showing compassion and care to your clients. It works in two easy steps:

One: full transparency and communication. Tell them exactly what happened, even if it's bad news for the case. Do not sugarcoat things.

Two: Tell them how sorry you are that X happened on the case, or that the case was lost, or, to an intake, that they have no case. Tell them that if it were up to you, you would go all the way to the Supreme Court (assuming the cause has merit, obviously). Tell them how much you want to help them but that there's an impossibility because of things beyond your control: the law is the way it is, the legal system is the way it is. Tell them the loss, or the situation, hurts you even more. That you would do anything in your power if there was something that could be done.

I have clients or potential clients I talk to where the message I've given them is simple: "Your case sucks." That's really the bottom line of my message to them. However, I say it in a way that even though I am telling them their case sucks, they still love me and the firm because they feel I care. They know that the reason we lost a case or can't take a case is because the law is a certain way and civil lawsuits have certain realities that make the case not viable; or some other extraneous—beyond your control—reason. But they know at the end of the day, that if it were up to me, I would pursue their case. If it were viable, I'd be all over it fighting by their side. These leads or clients, notwithstanding their disappointment at the moment, still come back with more cases of their own, or referrals of people from their network. Keep in mind each human being you talk to has a network of around 30 to 40 people. When you talk to any given human being, you are potentially, indirectly, reaching 30 or 40 others who may have a legal need.

KEEP SHARP

As a business owner, nobody is going to "train" you. Nobody is going to tell you that you suck. Your employees won't, certainly. Every year, some 4,000 new lawyers enter the Florida market, all hungrier than you. Some competent, some not. Some giving services at fees they shouldn't, at the expense of quality. But that's reality. You must go out there and compete. You don't take one single client for granted. You must keep your quality and sharpness up.

In this context, self-improvement is key. No time spent on self-improvement is wasted.

During my morning "concentration" time, I apportion some minutes to reading. It could be as little as 15 to 20 minutes. A chapter of some book. Over time, it accumulates and in two months, if you are consistent, you could have read an entire book. Half of more of what I read is non-law related stuff, and the other half is in some area of law I want to learn or improve. On the law side, I read textbooks, law review articles, the Florida Bar Journal, SCOTUS decisions, and other appellate decisions.

I also find it very important to explore other disciplines though. Topics of my interest are artificial intelligence, astrophysics, particle physics, neuroscience, psychology, self-improvement, calculus, philosophy, languages, and jurisprudence. I feel all that knowledge intersects. I've seen my little knowledge on thermodynamics applied to some aspects of cases. My few readings on neuroscience helped me anticipate an opposing counsel or judge's moves. My little knowledge of calculus helps me understand better the profitability of cases. I think, I said at the beginning of the book, that my non-law related readings inform many of my decisions as an attorney and businessman.

Though I am messy intellectually—I like to read about so many things—I always try to focus on something for a few months (3 to 6 months). The past three months for example (and the upcoming 3), I am seriously focused on becoming fluent in Portuguese. The semester before that, I was hyper focused on math. After I am done with Portuguese, I'll either go back to mathematics, physics, or jurisprudence. I haven't decided.

BE IN STORY MODE

Story telling is everything. Humans are wired to hear stories. Stories work with juries, with judges, with potential new clients, with employees, with everyone. If you are making videos online, speak in these videos with a story plot, with a beginning and end. In a world where there's a hypercomputation for people's attention, good story telling will set you apart. I practice story telling every day. I even like to tell my team stories about situation I've dealt with my clients. I try to make sure that whatever I am speaking has a beginning, a middle, and an end—like story.

SELF-AWARENESS

Self-awareness is key. Self-awareness is a weird thing. No one is perfectly self-aware. But you can tell those who are not self-aware. Usually those who think they are bigger-than-thou. Don't be that person that thinks he is 100, when he is 70. If you are that inaccurate about yourself, you are going to get hit hard when you play in the 100's league. There is, in my opinion, a self-awareness crisis. In psychology, the Dunning–Kruger effect is a cognitive bias in which people with low ability at a task overestimate their ability. Beware of the Dunning–Kruger effect. I've seen it live on myself.

I am all pro-overachieving and reaching for the stars. But you must do it with a good degree of self-awareness. It's a counterintuitive thing. If you feel less than what you are (but are ambitious) you will more likely achieve these ambitious goals because your "feeling less-ness" will make you work harder, and make sure you take care of every aspect of the game so you can compete in the major leagues.

I've always also been very insecure about myself. I've found, however, that my insecurity is good for litigation, especially at trial. As an insecure person, you want to control all aspects of the case, prepare for intangibles, and that makes for good trial practice where your plan goes out the window at every turn.

BEWARE OF BUYER'S PROCESS

Do not just be hungry and desperate for converting leads. **Buyers** of your product go through a process. Some don't even know yet that they need you. If you are just targeting those **buyers** ready to be converted into a lead, you are missing on a whole lot of **buyers**. Focus part of your marketing strategy in those who are still at the beginning of the process. Those who are in the "do I hire a lawyer or do I do it myself" type of situation.

Think of a small business owner who is starting to flourish (does not have a lawsuit pending, and therefore, does not need you now) but it is thinking that for compliance reasons, it may be a good idea to have an attorney. This small business owner is surveying the lawyer landscape online, still undecided if he even needs one. Think of what kind of content you are putting online (and the frequency) to make this person (1) think about you in the future, when he's ready or (2) bring him closer to the ready-to-be-converted lead stage. If you are interacting with a buyer at this stage in person, you may want to be careful and show him who you are as a person, rather than the sales-person lawyer eager to convert the lead. Build a pipeline of potential clients in each section of the **buyer's** path. Beginning (thinking about it, or do not know needs one), middle (knows he needs, but searching), end (ready to hire).

THE MILLIONAIRE TRAP AND RATES

In our line of business, regardless of what you do, just because you are an attorney, you are going to run into a successful wealthy person who will try to take advantage of you. They are going to approach you and try to get you to do free work for them. Silly things maybe. You, as a young practitioner, or just starting a practice, are going to do it, intimidated by this person's might and wealth (whose business you want badly) and do stuff here and there for free because in the back of your mind, this guy is going to end up bringing you the big case that makes you so much money and fixes your life.

WARNING!!! ** This is crap. ** I repeat, this is crap. It's a mirage. Don't let yourself be taken advantage of. We don't sell potatoes or tomatoes. We sell time. Discounts are ok. Free work for those who can pay, ABSOLUTELY NOT. You'll end up frustrated, broke, and the millionaire will end up taking the big work you wanted, to a big law firm. It has happened to me; it has happened to friends around me who own firms. Then, it happened to me, *again*, and *again*. Do not fall for this. I learned this the hard way. Today, we don't move a finger in a case (for a client who can or should pay) without first getting paid.

Now, that said, I would also advise you that you do more than what you get paid to do. If you got paid to work 5 hours, do 7. If you got paid to write a motion, include the reply too. Eventually, you will get paid more than what you actually do. If that person is the right client for you, they will see it, and will appreciate it. Then, later, as the trust is built, people will pay for the work, plus a premium for the care, for the relationship, for the compassion, for the trust, and for the peace of mind. That client will never leave you.

Don't overcharge either. Your value doesn't go to $1,000 an hour because you have 30 years of experience for the same product. A property case is a property case regardless of who's doing it, and it has a certain value. A 10-year practitioner's rate is not double the rate of a 5-year practitioner.

It is higher for the 10-year practitioner, but it is not double. There's also what the market pays for a given case. Even if you have such a relationship with your client that you can charge $2,000 an hour for a property claim, it would not be right. You are ripping that person off and you're messing up with market rates.

SOCIAL MEDIA

Social media could be the subject of an entire book. It is such a large topic and has virtually taken over all things marketing. I don't pretend to be an expert on social media. In fact, we have not been able to build a large following on any of our networks, but we are working on it, and while I do, a few things I have learned.

The first, is that your social media presence needs to match your brand. Even though I have to take some risks—otherwise you end up not posting anything—every video or post we do is done with the premise that it has to match our brand. That implies that you know your brand, of course. As a multitopic law firm we've defined our brand not glued to a practice area but to more abstract values such as a competent, quality-oriented representation that provides a value proposition. The better expression of it is what I tell all clients: we will never be the firm that charges you $100 to recover $100. We also associate our brand with honesty and care. We promise to be blunt and tell you the brutal truths others won't tell you just to take your money. We will tell you that your case sucks—no sugarcoating.

Every video I do (even every post in my personal account) has these ideas on the back of my mind. "How will it reflect on my brand" I always think before posting. I also try to balance that with the idea of posting a genuine version of myself, imperfect, not fake. I like the idea of "documenting" your life or who you are, more than "content creation." In the midst of the TikTok frenzy, and the brutal competition for leads, some attorneys think that all of a sudden, they have to be standup comedians. You don't. If you're not funny, don't try to be funny. It's the worst thing you can do. Nothing worse than forced humor.

Social media requires discipline. If you open an account and are going to post sporadically, you might as well not open it. The algorithm of most social platforms is brutal and will rank you higher the more continuous activity it detects. You have to be disciplined to constantly be posting content for your firm. You will never go viral with zero videos.

This year, we started experiencing with YouTube also. We are doing a biweekly podcast focused on interviewing law firm owners and other entrepreneurs. We have been very consistent. We are on Episode 14 (as of writing this) and consistency has brought us from 500-600 views on average to over 2,000. Our content is simple, genuine, and tries to provide insight into what it takes to make a law firm or other small enterprises. It also showcases the life of the entrepreneur so people can see the type of person they need to be if they want to be in business.

TAKE RISKS

I've had to take many risks as a solo practitioner, and later as the owner of a small uncapitalized firm. I've taken cases I had no idea how to do because I simply could not reject the income stream. I've taken cases against large firms that really knew what they were doing. But don't fear the large firms. They really know what they are doing, but so could you! If you read, study, and train, you can beat them. The top 100 tennis players in the world, in a given day, could beat Novak Djokovic. It is kind of the same. It's all about accumulating knowledge, organizing it well, and presenting it nicely to persuade a human being. Most jurors and judges can't handle overloads of information anyway!

Here and there, take on a case you don't know; it will make you a better lawyer.

GET THAT DEPOSIT

When you go to a store to buy furniture or things that require credit, people want to get you signed-in with a down payment, even if small. Once you are locked in, and the money is deposited, the likelihood of backing down goes down dramatically. If you've ever booked a cruise trip, you know this. They ask you for a very small deposit compared to the overall price of the trip.

Our business is no different. Get that deposit. If the intake walks out the door without that deposit, he'll be exposed to a dozen other lawyers, or could have a change of heart. Lock down deals. Of course, if you get that deposit, and they change their mind, and you did nothing in the case—it happens—refund 100% of it. Don't be that lawyer. Fees are never "non-refundable" despite what your retainer says. Fees are earned. You still have to refund unearned parts of deposits.

HOW TO SELECT CASES (Litigation)

1. The first element of a good case is a <u>compelling story</u>. If the story is just OK, it'll become bad when you hear the other side.

2. Are there <u>damages</u>? If there aren't, we are going to have to charge the person some of the fees. This makes the case likely not viable from a plaintiff's standpoint, and difficult from a defense perspective as well.

3. <u>Collectability</u>. You need a defendant with deep pockets. If the case is meritorious (#1), and has damages (#2), but there isn't a good, collectable defendant, the case will not be viable. 95% of clients will not take that risk, nor will we recommend it.

4. Do you have a good <u>witness/partner</u>? The plaintiff <u>IS</u> the case. We must assess, from the start, the credibility, commitment, personality, intelligence, and communication skills of the main witness in the case.

5. Are there good, typical, commonly filed <u>causes of action</u>? We have to rapidly identify causes of action that are common, that do not get dismissed, and that do not require difficult things to prove like reliance, intent, etc.

6. Are there favorable <u>case decisions</u> similar to our fact pattern in our jurisdiction? The law of the jurisdiction matters. For example, on TCPA cases (unwanted text and calls cases), the 11th Circuit requires that defendants send multiple texts. Other circuits are OK with just one text.

SEE LIFE AS A UNITY

It's been many years now that I see life as a unity. Though I do believe in the notion of "work-life balance," I tend to think, even on my downtime, about the firm. How does this tennis match help me be a better leader of the firm, I ask myself. Well, cardio workouts are good for the heart, which then better pumps out blood to my brain, which then makes it operate better, which makes me then a better decision-maker, which makes me then a better leader. As crazy as it sounds, I think these things.

Tennis, my favorite hobby, is also very competitive. The competitiveness of it, I like to think, helps me be more competitive in my cases. Tennis also requires quick, reflexive reactions. I like to think (though I have no evidence of it) that that reactiveness of tennis helps me be better reactive in my practice and business, which requires quick reactions and quick decisions daily.

Everything you do, look at it as furthering your firm. Make the firm your life's goal. Your family, sports, your reads, etc. It will also help you select your hobbies better, and I believe, it will make you better in both your professional and your personal life.

ETHICS

Ethics can be hard. I've had two Florida Bar complaints from clients. One of them was frivolous and was easily dismissed. The other one, I mentioned it earlier in the book, involved an inadvertent error that after some clarification to the Bar authorities, was also dismissed. Both of these things happened within the 3 years after being admitted. Compliance with ethics rules can be everything but straightforward. The pressure to make money, week after week, month after month, can put you in a position where you are vulnerable to mistakes. It's not the same handling one case than handling 100 cases. The sheer volume, without the proper organization, systems, discipline, and hard work, will make you prone to errors.

Representation can also face you with inherent conflicts. Conflicts when you represent people that are close, or when you are in the middle of transactions with many parties involved. Conflicts are not apparent all the time. You have to learn to spot the conflicts, and to see if the conflict is curable (via written disclosure and waiver), or if it's a conflict that will require you to let go of the case (and deprive you from that much needed income).

Since my first bar complaint, I have an ethics lawyer on retainer. I've found it the best practice. Whenever I face a complicated client or situation, I email my ethics lawyer for guidance on how to proceed. At least, you are acting under the advice of counsel, even if you get it wrong.

CLIENT EDUCATION

It is very important for you to learn to educate clients. Eight out of ten clients do not want to pay for the intangible product we sell: time. They hate it. They are cheap. They want discounts. You have to teach them, especially those clients that become more established, that what you sell is time, and that they get none of your time prior to payment. It can be challenging. But with time, they will learn. One of my first corporate clients, dating back to early 2014, used to be the cheapest guy in the world. God, the guy was so hard to collect from. He wanted free legal advice all the time. It got to a point where, respectfully, I would tell him: "John, I am not moving a finger until you deposit money in our accounts." I did this every time he needed something. With time, we are not only great friends now, but he appreciates my time and work more than ever. You would think that because he's my friend now, he would be even worse at paying and expect free stuff. On the contrary. Now we have that perfect balance where he values my friendship and work, and that my work is remunerated.

* * *

A HELL OF A CASE

In the earlier parts of this book, I walked you through some of the things I went through in order to start and build Ayala Law. Now, I want to give you fine-tuned details of a real-life experience of what it takes to build a litigation firm with no money, no resources, no connections, no writing skills, no talent for oral argument, or, at best, a very tiny little amount of each of these. Obviously, there were some dollars in my account, even if not enough to pay for experts. I have some oratory talent, even if not enough to persuade certain federal judges. I have some writing skills, even if not enough to be published in law review circles. Etcetera. You get the idea. I can go down the list and I can assure you that I am, in every item, average at best.

It was early in 2017. I don't recall exactly what month, maybe February or March. I was still living at a tiny 400 square feet studio in Brickell House, a nice building in Brickell, Miami, a block from my office. I always thought living super close to the office was important for success. Commuting time is wasted time. Before 2017, I had been getting a lot of business from Peter, a close friend from high school that had become a successful businessman in Peru and internationally. Part of my work with him involved implementing his businesses here in the U.S. South America and the U.S. are more connected than you may think. There's a lot of things happening that intersect the two. From plenty of import and export transactions to real estate investments. Purchases of U.S. equipment, conference travel, pleasure travel, you name it. This intense interconnection generates a lot of legal work.

Peter had a lot of connections. He has introduced me to a lot of good business contacts. He would always give me the heads up: Edwards—as he calls me—I am giving your number to X who has some issue in the U.S. to see if you can help him. I would thank him and patiently wait for the new contact (new business opportunity) call. You have to understand that to seal the deal on a case, especially a case where the client gives you something between 5K-10K retainer is not a matter of one call. They make a first contact with you, and you give them X impression. They then go around talking to other attorneys for a second opinion. Then they go around and talk to people who may know you. They then look you up online, and then, they call you again and then you may seal the deal. On occasions, a third or fourth meeting/call is required to seal the deal.

At Brickell House, there was no self-parking. You had to forcibly valet. I remember I was dropping my car at the valet when I get this call from an area code that appeared to be from Peru. I answer the call and it was Willy. I had already met Willy at a social event in Peru a year or so ago through Peter. But we had not spoken at length. Willy was the CEO of medium size agricultural company in Peru. Agriculture is big in Peru. Willy tells me about this situation where he purchased pea seeds from a California company. The seeds were rotten and ruined all his fields and crops for the season. Agriculture is a tricky business. You put a disease in one part of the land and depending on what it is, it can spread meteorically and ruin all your lands for that season. Willy also told me some of the more technical details about what had happened, which I tried to grasp fast to make me seem knowledgeable. One key fact he told me was that another Peruvian grower had also purchased the same batch of seeds from the same seller in California. The other grower's lands were in an area completely opposite from where Willy had his lands.

I knew nothing about agricultural litigation, federal litigation, seed law (there's something called the Federal Seed Act, believe it or not), California law, warranty laws, or the agricultural industry in general—*nothing*. But my intuition (and plain logic) told me that it was a good case. If the same seeds caused the same effect to two different growers, one to the south, one to the north, in different geographic climates, what are the chances the seeds did not cause the problem? Moreover, both growers were experienced and had a good track record as growers. I don't believe back in early 2017—six years ago—I had a good grasp at how hard litigation is; even when the facts are on your side. I did not know well how brutal it can be to go against well-resourced large firms even when most of the facts are favorable. They find bad facts and convert the good ones into just OK ones. In my mind, I had a great case—I don't care what the law says, I thought, there had to be a case.

Somehow, despite my ignorance and lack of experience, I was able to persuade Willy, in my first call, that I was the right guy for the case. One of my sale pitches techniques in medium to big cases has always been to attack big law. I'll say things like "Willy, if you hire a big firm, they are going to charge you like crazy for what? We all went to the same schools; we all have the same degree. It's about how much you are willing to put in the work." The idea we will work hard on the case and relentlessly pursue justice, coupled with how overprized and overrated big law lawyers are, has had good marketing results for me when closing deals.

As a result of my successful call with Willy, he was going to arrange a meeting with me and Omar, the other grower. Omar was the owner of a 20+ years old family-owned company. Omar's business was larger than Willy's, probably by a factor of three or four. They had purchased even more seed bags from the California grower and therefore had more damages.

Omar was intelligent, articulate, and knowledgeable in agriculture. Like most businessmen, Omar talks a lot. I would listen to his story and made a pitch to him similar to the one I made to Willy. I don't recall the details, but I think the call went well. To my benefit, Omar had already paid a big firm in California to analyze the case, even though he did not tell me at the time. So, my "big law is overrated" narrative must have resounded well with him.

Later, we had a call with both of them, where I offered joint representation. I explained to them the pros and cons of jointly representing them. They loved the idea, especially because they could jointly finance the case and make it viable. They were both broke because of the rotten California seeds situation.

I don't recall at what point, but for sure before signing him officially as a client, Omar showed me the California firm memorandum of law. They believed there was a case but that overcoming some warranty and disclaimer issues—necessary to have access to the larger set of damages, as opposed to a mere refund of the seed price—was going to be a difficult proposition. I kind of disagreed with their research. My research showed that we were going to be able to overcome that and go to a jury. Mind you, however, I am very bad at research; they were probably right. (You'll know what happened soon enough).

Omar had paid a fortune for that silly memo. Generally, I am not a believer, with some exceptions, on these memoranda of law. I think they make litigation expensive. In my firm we are more agile. "Ryan, what does the case law show on X topic?" Ryan gets the case, I read it, and boom, we know what's going on. We quickly know what to advise the client. Hey, but at least I had the benefit of that memo of law. To me, if that big firm believed there could be a case—even if it were a tough road ahead—then I was right in pursuing it. Tough roads are not a problem for me at all. The idea that it was hard attracted rather than repelled me.

I don't recall what I told Omar. I think I told him the legal opinion of the big firm was correct, but that the case was still doable. That the problem they had was that they charged overpriced hours, that that factored in their opinion, and he'd have to finance the entire case with them. With me, I could offer a hybrid monthly flat-fee and contingency that would make the case financially viable. Mind you, when you do mostly plaintiff work, the client is always broke. They come to you to sue somebody because somebody has taken from them, created losses, and put them in a bad financial position. The last thing they want is to pay exorbitant legal fees—or any fees at all. Though I have taken some risky litigation on contingency, this was not a case I could take on a pure contingency basis. I asked them both to pay a $10,000 monthly fee as long as the case lasted. They negotiated it down to $5,000, which was my bottom line. For me, a broke firm, 5K a month was almost like 15% or 20% of my budget back then. The idea of having that stream of income for the foreseeable years was attractive—even if the case intimidated me a little bit. I had never done a federal case, let alone one in California. They also had to cover all the costs. I would also take 20% of whatever I could recover at any time.

I had no idea what to do. I was still not as good at litigation in general. My first jury trial—the first time I saw a litigation case through—was in mid-2018. But for some reason, perhaps because of my philosophy training, I have this idea that everything, absolutely everything in life, stems from basic, logical principles. I believe that everything is understandable. I am also—I have to say, in one of those rare instances I compliment myself—brave. I am rarely afraid. What's the worst that can happen? I always think. Somebody loses money? I lose a case? I lose money? I get disbarred? None of these things involve life or death. You can recover from all of these. You can't recover from death.

I had not hired Luis Quesada yet. Luis is one of the smartest people I've ever met. And he came to handle the California case writing load almost entirely. So, I had to deal with the case myself at the beginning. As usual, I start from the basics. I started reading about federal practice, the federal rules of civil procedure, looking up federal complaints and federal dockets, etc. Informing myself as to how the hell federal cases go about.

I drafted what I thought was a very good complaint. I had a lot of help from Oscar, who is detailed oriented and had a good team. His team had documented the situation well and wrote internal memos which were the basis for the factual section of my complaint. To a lesser degree, Willy's company had done something similar. When I saw what these two little Peruvian companies had done, their professionalism, it made me proud (not only as a Peruvian) but made me proud to fight for them and get these crooked California growers to pay for selling—fully aware—rotten seeds.

I reviewed what I wrote many times. I had no one to help me. The case did not pay enough to bring in co-counsel. Splitting 5K was going to drain all my profits. I needed this income to have some stability in my payroll.

I still needed to find local counsel in California to get me admitted pro hac vice there. I had done the research and I felt confident that we were not going to be subject to arbitration. My research also showed that we were solid in the Central District of California, in Los Angeles, venue wise. I thought that I should find a small, solo practitioner. Someone I could tell what to do and that would not mess around with my case. If the guy had a partner or was part of a big firm, there would be bureaucracy involved, everyone would challenge my judgment, and perhaps realize I didn't know what I was doing. I couldn't deal with that. That's why I started my firm after all, not to have 10 people destroy my papers.

In my Google search, I found this solo practitioner named Bob. Bob is of Asian descent (as many in California). He had gone to a good school and graduated with honors. In what was surprising to me, he did not go the big law—or even medium practice—path, but dedicated himself to a high-volume bankruptcy, form-type of practice. He had hundreds of Chapter 7 and Chapter 13 consumer petitions and that's all he did. He appeared to be happy with that. It's crazy how what would make one miserable (myself) makes another man happy. It's a matter of suitability, and that is the essence of this book, to try to show you how to build a firm suitable to you.

Bob had very little social skills. It was almost odd at times to interact with him. He did not care to meet me, know who I was, or my background. It was kind of perfect for what I needed, but odd. He charged me only his billable hours—which were minimal—and was comfortable with me doing all the work, which again, is what I wanted. Not all lawyers will agree to that. Lawyers are difficult, complicated people. The first thing they think is: what if you screw up in the case and my name is on the line. I find the average lawyer to be a very defensive, risk adverse person. I don't know if Bob searched me, but he did not bring any of these concerns up.

Long story short, I was admitted to the Central District of California and ready to file my case.

The first thing that I screwed up was format. I read the local rules and the federal rules of procedure forwards and backwards, and I honestly did not run into any particular format requirements. As it turns out, there was one. California cases are all written in a certain style. The more salient feature is they write their papers with two sort of numbered rulers on the sides that count the line numbers. Sort of like a deposition transcript. Font and spacing is also regulated. I first noticed this when I saw the first filing from the defense. I was a little embarrassed but undeterred. Throughout my life, literally, in everything I've done, I've managed to do things in a way that even when I screw up, I don't screw up in a gigantic way that ruins something irreversibly. I've always had that premise on the back of my mind. This new case was no exception.

Federal litigation is different. There is this Rule 16 conference and Rule 26 disclosures that were not common in state court. They are more so now, but they weren't back then. I remember that my research showed that I had to meet with the attorneys from the two defendants. I initially sued the seller of the seeds only. Later I amended the complaint and added the manufacturer of the seeds. I should have done this from the beginning, but I thought that lack of privity with the manufacturer prevented me from suing it. This is the world of products liability. It's kind of like suing Chevrolet and the Chevy dealer that sold you the car. The manufacturer was a Washington State, fairly big and old corporation. The seller was this one-man shop, long time seed broker who also happened to be an attorney. As plaintiffs, we were more interested in the manufacturer's deeper pockets.

The manufacturer hired a long-time agricultural litigator. The guy professed himself to be an expert in seed litigation. I was not impressed, but because of my inexperience in litigation in general—especially federal—and my lack of familiarity with agricultural litigation, I always worked under the assumption that Dale (that was his name) knew a lot. The lawyer for the seller was appointed by the insurance company. Sam was his name. He worked for a 20-plus lawyer firm in Los Angeles that mainly did insurance defense work. Sam was a great guy. We became friends with time even if litigation was contentious. I could tell he hated his job. He hated defending insurance companies, but like most lawyers, he did it because it paid decently well. He sacrificed happiness for money. I don't judge him. He was a good guy. Later, towards the end of the case, he went to a smaller firm of one of his law school buddies, where I believe he partnered with him. I had respect for Sam. I think he was intellectually solid.

Because I was unfamiliar with this Rule 16 meeting, I thought it had to be a real meeting. So, I led the coordination, scheduled the meeting, and booked my flights to California. The meeting was going to be held at the defense firm's main office in Ventura. When I got there, five lawyers in a conference room were waiting for me. They were all surprised I flew all the way there for a Rule 16 meeting. I tried to sound experienced, and I said something like "I love in person meetings, and I love traveling. I don't mind getting on a plane." I've done dozens of federal cases since then, and I now know that this meet and confer can be a call, or even email exchange—if a given court order does not require an actual conversation. I think that that is the only in person Rule 16 meeting I've ever had in a case. It's been mostly emails and some calls since.

The defense (and their clients) kind of knew that I did not know what I was doing and that played to my advantage. They underestimated me. They underfunded the case, blew all sorts of discovery deadlines, and were in a difficult position for trial. Both sides took about 3-4 depositions. Though they insinuated they would do it, they never got around to visit the plaintiffs' lands in Peru. This would have been important for them as their defense—*ad nauseam*—hinged over the idea that the plaintiffs did not know what they were doing. Other defenses included that Peruvian lands were contaminated, Peruvian water had bacteria, or that Peruvian agricultural practices in general are not clean or professional. They were silly, stupid defenses manufactured out of thin air. They had no foundation in fact. But as I have learned over time, defense counsel is skillful at manufacturing alternative theories, hammering on them over and over, and presenting the manufactured theory in a creative, persuasive way that creates doubt in the adjudicator—jury or judge. I underestimated their ability to do this in this case.

The first big hurdle we faced was motions to dismiss (MTDs). More accustomed to state work, I was a little overconfident in our ability to defeat these MTDs. Later, I'd learned that in federal court a lot of cases are thrown out at the motion to dismiss stage. We briefed the motions back. I say we, but really, Luis did. By now, I already had Luis at the firm. He was literally my savior. He defeated them. I owe him so much. I know he knows. I was only in charge to argue what he wrote. It was my first time arguing in federal court, in California, in one of the most important courts in the world. For those who don't know, a lot of high profile, civil rights, election, and political cases are addressed there. If I had to describe a talent, it would be perhaps the fact that I have the balls to go to unknown, intimidating places. I don't lack fear, but fear does not paralyze me.

Anyhow, I had to go argue the motions. I studied like it was the Florida Bar exam. I didn't know what to expect. I booked my flight and a hotel near the courthouse. As usual, I was sleep deprived. As a small practitioner, you do all this while having to take care of 10 other things in the firm, including payroll. You have to make sure that there's always money for payroll. People must eat. You also have a personal life, a partner to take care of. But anyhow, nothing a Red Bull or espresso can't fix. I woke up very early at the hotel to review my argument. I've always been an early riser. That's about the only time my brain works well—if at all.

My hotel was at walking distance from the courthouse. I had already calculated that the day before in Google Maps. I've always been a punctual person. I always get to places early enough to account for unexpected contingencies. If there was an unusually long line to go through security, it doesn't matter. I am always early enough to account for that, especially for important events. Same with airports. I am a 3-hours before (for international flights) and a 2-hours before (for domestic flights) type of guy.

The courthouse was grandiose. This magnificent glass covered modern building with 20 feet floors or higher. The entire building occupied an entire square block. Federal courthouses are like that. The feds have so much money; nothing compared to state courthouses. Although the building has only about 12 floors, each floor height is so high that it appears really large. As you walk in, you can see from the bottom to the last floor and ceiling of the entire building. The floors all have an inner edge corridor where you can see the bottom lobby from each of them. My courtroom was on the 8th floor. All the outside walls of the courtrooms are covered in nicely polished wooden finish. It all looks really like a high-end mall.

Outside, I ran into opposing counsel. As we were waiting for the court to open up in fixed benches against the wall right outside, the judge's main clerk, Mr. Tin, comes out with copies of a "draft decision" on the motion. He essentially told us that that was the judge's tentative ruling, and when we came in, to approach the podium as we were called with any disagreements we had with the ruling. All counsel started reading the beautifully crafted ruling. In federal court, writing is done at the highest of levels. It's a thing of beauty. It's what I love the most about federal practice.

The Court's tentative ruling kept alive three out of five of our causes of action against the moving defendant. I was completely cool with it. Like my good friend Andrew Bernhard (and one of the smartest lawyers I know) said once, in this business, you only need one cause of action, and win on it. I had three. The two knocked down were what we thought were the weakest anyway. I told Mr. Tin that I was not going to challenge the Court's tentative ruling. I then spoke to opposing counsel for the seed seller, with whom I had a great relationship. I told him it was going to be hard to get rid of a case with so many factual issues at this stage. He got rid of the counts with intent components— the ones alleging their client did what they did on purpose. I told him he should accept it. He didn't agree. He said he was going to challenge it. I thought it was a bad idea for him.

A few minutes later we were called inside the courthouse. The courthouse was also magnificent. One of the largest courthouses I've ever been to. Wooden interiors and super modern computer systems with screens all over the place for jurors to see evidence. The judge's place was an at least six feet high structure overlooking all of us from afar. The judge then called the case on the record. She asked that if someone was challenging the tentative ruling, they should approach the podium. Counsel for the seed seller approaches. He starts making his argument, he was a little flustered, to be honest. It got to an embarrassing point when as he's arguing against the order, he tells the judge (a very serious Asian woman) something along the lines of: "I know Your Honor's opinion is that negligence applies but ... [some other argument]." The judge flipped on him and said something like: "Mr. Chen, I don't provide opinions, I make rulings. Tell me what's wrong with my ruling based on precedent you can cite; otherwise, I suggest you move on to other topics or accept my ruling on negligence." Mr. Chen moved on to other topics, but shortly after had to go back to his chair. I don't practice often in this court, but I could tell the "tentative" part of the tentative ruling was decorative. The tentative ruling is the ruling, and I highly doubt that many attorneys are able to reverse that with oral argument.

It was a big win for me, my team, and my client. Even though clients don't truly appreciate much surviving a motion to dismiss and how hard it can be. Nine out of ten clients have a "why haven't we won the case yet" attitude. The lack of understanding of the litigation process (especially rules of evidence), coupled with a one-sided version of the events makes them believe that their case is a slam-dunk win.

We moved on to discovery. The other side continued to underestimate me. They really sat on the case and let me drive it. I've always had a litigation philosophy that you cannot spend a million dollars to win a million dollars. As basic as this principle sounds, it is inapplicable to the defense industry. They spend a million dollars to later pay a million dollars in a settlement—*all the time*. As a plaintiff's attorney though, I am always faced with a party who has been wronged. Someone has taken from my client, and, as a result, they are broke. The last thing they want is to pay legal fees. Yes, in the perfect world you should take 50 depositions and know what every single potential witness will say at trial. But that is rarely viable unless you are a big law firm representing a big defendant that simply wants to out-gas you (and feed your law firm's bottom line). Most of the time, it is my experience, you can have a pretty good idea of what a witness will say, even without a deposition. Since nine out of ten cases settle, I have very little incentive to take many depositions that will never be used. You will find that a lot of lawyers disagree with me on this. Most lawyers take—assuming budget is decent—as many depositions as possible. Some would say these have a big impact on settlement—I disagree. They do impact, though not a lot. To me, depositions are one of the things that make litigation expensive the most. Transcripts alone can be thousands of dollars—let alone attorney time preparing and taking (or defending) the deposition.

The defense underestimating me benefited me. They continued to blow off discovery deadlines as we were fast approaching trial. In this business, normally (with exceptions), the plaintiff wants to go to trial, and the defendant wants to drag the case out forever.

One key deadline was expert disclosure. I had never dealt with experts in federal court. The federal rule required that your expert disclose a report with his opinions on the case—what he will say at trial. I did not have a budget for experts. But I had heard already from the defense that they were going to bring five experts to the case. So, I told the clients that—as broke as they were—they had to come up with money for experts. I told them we needed at least two: a plant pathologist and a damages expert (a forensic accountant). Based on my trial experience up to then, I knew that these were the minimum experts we'd need if we wanted to have a decent shot at winning the case. I stressed the point to the clients: "if you guys want to win this, we need experts." Thankfully, they cared a lot about recovering in their case, and they came through. I had a damages expert I had used in prior trials—David Cowheard. He was not that expensive. Though he had no expertise in agriculture or fresh produce, I trusted that he was intellectually solid and that he'd be a great expert witness. He had been qualified as a damages expert in many courts already.

The plant pathologist was a much harder endeavor. A plant pathologist is essentially a plant doctor. There aren't many of these in the U.S. Think about it, who wants to be a doctor for plants? Most of these you find at research universities. I reached out to more than a dozen. Three reactions I got: (1) they ignored me; (2) they didn't want to be part of a legal case where they had to take a position that would make them seem they were not a neutral scientist; or (3) they couldn't do it because of their work at universities or with the government. I also found this one expert, very reputable, that was perfect for the job and who routinely testified in courts. When I contacted him, he declined. The reason? He had already been contacted by the defense.

The deadline was fast approaching, and I had no one with most simply ignoring me. Through more Google searches, I found Dr. Michael Coffey. Dr. Coffey was quite the character. During my first call with him, he quickly bought into the case's basic premise: if two very experienced growers, one in the south, one in the north, in areas with very different climates, who planted the same batch of seeds obtained the exact same result, it is highly unlikely that the fields or agricultural practices were the cause of the damage. The more logical conclusion was that the seeds were bad. Some of the issues I had with Dr. Coffey were his advanced age, that he talked nonstop, and his lack of familiarity with computers. He was—then—82 years old and still wrote things in pen and paper. The guy was brilliant, however. One of the smartest humans I've ever met. He had everything, including all sorts of chemical formulas recorded in his brain. I would send him research papers about the topic, he would read them in minutes, and talk about them in depth. He had—he said—a photographic memory. He did not read words but big blocks, which were then easy for him to memorize. He is a genius. He would talk to me in a level of sophistication that was very hard for me to keep up. Like most geniuses, he doesn't understand that normal humans process things at different speeds than his brain. He was funny, charismatic, casual, and relaxed. I thought the jury would find him very likeable. He agreed to do the work. He did not ask for a big retainer. It was great. I had my plant pathologist.

Now and then though, he would get lost. He would not answer my calls for days on important moments in the case. Moments when we had to submit reports or present expert affidavits to rebut motions. He really gave me a few scares—including a massive one at trial, which I'll tell you about in a bit.

Another key deadline in the case was the summary judgment deadline. For non-lawyers, summary judgment is a motion that aims to win the case before trial. Unlike the motion to dismiss, evidence is allowed to be considered in summary judgment motions. I knew the older lawyer for the seed manufacturer did not have it in him to do all the work that a motion for summary judgment required (plus, he had done no discovery, what was he going to say?). The lawyer for the seed seller did tell me he was going to file one. The court had very cumbersome and strict procedures for summary judgment motions that made them very laborious. The day of the deadline, Mr. Chen filed all his summary judgment papers, the motion and the required memorandum of points and authorities in support of the motion. It was massive work. The insurance company must have easily paid twenty or thirty grand on that motion work.

We now had the massive work of opposing it. Needless to say, Luis took the lead on all this work. Luis is one of the most detail-oriented persons I've ever met. I think in a four-year span I've found one typo in his work. It's insane. His eyes see through words different than normal humans. I don't really correct his work—he's the authority at the firm when it comes to legal writing. But I do read some of them (especially in our big cases) because I have now many years of oral argument experience and I know a little bit about what arguments sell better to judges. I also have a decent strategic mind so I might tell him, hey, let's make this line of argument. Most of the time though, his papers are filed untouched. It also helps that—with certain differences—we agree on the fundamentals of the arguments. Partly because he's very docile to adapt to what he thinks are the things or ideas I like, and partly because I believe that we both have very solid logical foundations; mine through my philosophical training, his, I'd say, God given, natural.

In federal court, days when you have to file big papers are brutal. I remember we stayed late (which we never do) to finish filing and adjusting all the affidavits, exhibits, and papers. Remember, that, in the middle of all our other work.

Fast forward a bit, and I had to go argue against the motion in California. I did not expect that this was going to be as easily defeated as the motion to dismiss. If a lot of cases are gotten rid of at the motion to dismiss stage in federal court, a lot more than that are defeated at the summary judgment stage. I had to be very careful. Like for the other motion, I had overprepared. I knew my argument very well, even if I always have a feeling that I could have prepared more—that feeling is never absent. But I knew things well. I wasn't sure if this was going to be like the other time where the clerk came out of the courtroom to hand us a tentative ruling but, as it turns out, it was the same. The tentative ruling denied the motion for summary judgment. The judge thought that there were enough factual issues for the case to go to the jury. One of the main things we overcame was the defense's argument that the "economic loss rule" prevented us from recovering on non-contractual theories of liability—which we needed in order to get more than a mere refund of the seed price. We defeated the seed seller's arguments as to the economic loss rule, for now. It would not be the end of the economic loss rule attacks, as you will see later.

The case was to go to trial in February 2020. A couple of weeks before trial, the seed manufacturer hired a new firm. They got rid of the old man who had pretty much tanked their case. As is usual, their new counsel wanted a continuance. I was extremely opposed to a continuance. The case was becoming very difficult to finance for both clients after 3 years. They were missing their monthly payments. They were behind like 3 months then, I remember. Business-wise, if I'm not collecting payments, my only choice is to push the case to trial as fast as possible. That way, the defense—faced with the possibility of a trial they may lose—is more inclined to settle the case. We had gone to two mediation sessions to no avail, with no reasonable offers from either defendant. For us, any chance at settlement would have had to be in the seven figures, and even that may not have made it. My clients were alleging millions of dollars in lost profits and truly believed in their case—even accounting for me explaining how difficult it would be to get a seven-figure verdict. I thought we could reach a seven-figure verdict. However, a multimillion verdict—what they wanted—would be much more difficult. In most cases commercial cases—it's my experience—the hard part is to prove damages, not liability.

The new counsel—from a big law firm—pushed hard to persuade me to a short continuance. I am all for civility and reasonable concessions in litigation. So, I agreed to a short 4-week continuance as long as the court had availability. When we submitted the joint motion, the court set the trial not for March but April 2020, about eight weeks from what we requested. The court wanted the case gone too; it had been on its docket for too long. Not what I wanted, but not that bad either. Eight weeks is nothing in our business. Who would have thought, though, that in March 2020, a worldwide pandemic would hit, and my trial would be indefinitely postponed. And remember, this is California we are talking about—if you know what I mean. I was utterly deflated. The firm's business model relies on income from small cases: immigration, small litigation retainers, real estate closings, small settlements, and others. But once or twice a year, we need to hit some bigger pot to finance the firm. The small fees generally do not cover the firm's expenses. We usually rely on three sources of financing: (1) my personal savings; (2) lines of credit from banks; (3) cash we have from bigger payout cases. In February 2020, the firm was starving for a payout. On top of that, not only were the clients behind on their monthly payments, but I couldn't possibly charge them five thousand dollars a month during a period of the case where I was not going to move a finger. So, we had to readjust our agreement. In short, the financial implications of the delay were big. If you add to that that, during the pandemic, there was no business, things get even worse.[19]

After several status conferences, and tentative dates for trial, trial was finally set for the third week of June 2021—about 14 months later. This

---

[19] The pandemic was an extremely challenging time for the firm financially. One of the things I am always concerned about—besides having money to pay our bills—is that the team has things to do. When the team does not have things to do, a feeling of "things are not right" at the firm may spread. When they are busy, and if they trust you, they feel that money is coming in one way or another. The last thing you want is your team deflated, low in confidence in the firm's financial health. The team wants stability; if they don't feel it, they'll start searching for other options. This situation is what made me start an illegal towing practice. I had already been doing towing cases since 2016, but when the pandemic hit, we brought it to the next level. We literally filed probably more than 100 towing cases. One of the easiest ways to sign cases is free cases. Nobody likes to pay. When you tell someone, "Yes, I'll represent you for free, you don't have to pay anything," everybody signs. Add to that the new Zoom court reality and we were able to sue towing companies state-wide. We created systems, processes, and all of a sudden, we had a volume illegal towing practice. The practice did not turn out to be very profitable, though. But hey, at least it kept us busy, did some good, and brought some dollars. The best thing, I believe (because there's something positive in every situation), we became illegal towing experts. I don't believe anyone in Florida knows more towing law than we do. That expertise we can use now more wisely and selectively. We sign better cases and settle them (or win) for better dollars. We also have a reputation. When you are the authority in the area, cases settle for more money. I love our towing practice. My towing clients are some of the best clients I've had, and helping them, fills my heart with joy.

time it was game time. The judge wanted to get rid of our case (it was a four-year-old case then) and even offered more mediation sessions with federal judges from other divisions to no avail. Our clients, especially one of them, had gone through hell with the situation. The family business had nearly been destroyed because of the rotten seeds. It was very emotional for them. There was a "they have to pay for what they did" feeling that would get in the way of more moderate, viable settlements.

The preparations for trial began. One of the things they don't teach in law school—among many—is trial logistics. Trial is literally like organizing an event: a party, a concert, or a show. I don't see any difference from the logistics standpoint. The amount of coordination, on what was really a medium size case, is insane. I had to get all my witnesses lined up. Make sure they didn't have any conflicts. Make sure also that they were available for the entire trial period, even if they were going to speak for an hour. Make flight and hotel arrangements. (Remember, a lot of witnesses were in Peru, and we had to fly them from there). Make arrangements for myself, my co-counsel, and Luis. Print thousands and thousands of pages, tabulate them, put them in binders, all in a pretty and organized way that's easily accessible at trial. Coordinate this with the defense, who is going to object to 1,000 things in what you printed. Coordinate with the court regarding equipment and technology. Bring digital equipment of our own. Get case law ready for evidence challenges—you bet they're coming. Trial logistics are hell. It is a show where there are so many moving parts, and you have to make sure all the details are perfectly lined up for performance time— the trial. I don't have a formula. I am not a pro at trial logistics or at logistics in general. My approach is very basic: I make lists, schedules, outlines, tasks, and calendars—as much as I can.

We were finally there. We traveled more than a week in advance to meet with all witnesses and prep them. I went with Jorge Garcia-Menocal, who is like my brother, with whom I've done nearly all my jury trials. We make a great team. He's a fantastic trial attorney. Although we are about the same age, and we treat each other as equals, he's a bit of a mentor to me when it comes to trial.

The first days, the goal was to prepare all the witness questionnaires. Direct examination is really like a show. The more in detail you prepare the questions and practice them, the better it will go. You want to get all the facts of your story out in an organized, storytelling way without falling into narrative testimony. For this to work, you have to practice with the witness. We had around ten witnesses (5 on each side), so it was a lot of work. Time was also a problem. Our judge assigned only 9 hours of testimony for each side. Opening, closing, and other things did not count. We had a 5-day trial only. Both sides had requested eight days. We had already done our research on this judge, and we knew that she was going to use a timer and keep us to our 9 hours. She was as strict a judge as it gets.

The defense had around 9 witnesses, 5 of which were experts we didn't get to depose. We really did not have the resources to undertake these depositions. We never thought they would call them all. We underestimated them. They brough all five to trial, and they all passed through the witness stand one by one. That's all their case really consisted of, as I'll explain later.

Jury selection was fairly simple. In federal court, jury selection time is minimal. In state court, you can get an entire day for jury selection. Here, the judge had already given us pre-written questions and we knew we only had 20 minutes each to ask follow-up questions or additional questions of our own that couldn't repeat or be similar to the judge's questions. Jorge, as in all our trials, took the lead on jury selection. Jorge is extremely likeable and having him be the first to interact with the jurors—I feel—sets a good tone. Given the limitations in time, we really couldn't have much of an impact one way or the other. We needed to select 8 jurors—per the court's rule. They would all stay throughout trial and then, before going to deliberate, two would be released. We selected what we thought was a good panel that we thought would favor us as the underdog at trial.

We had settlement offers all the way up to trial day. The clients rejected them all. One of the latest offers would end up being higher than the outcome at trial. But that's just life. We simply couldn't have anticipated it.

Once the jury was ready and the instructions given, I was up for opening statements. I don't like opening statements because by rule you are limited as to what you are allowed to say. You cannot be argumentative but only speak as to what the evidence will show. I was extremely prepared. I had my entire script down word for word, but I also memorized it by sections and ideas so I could speak without a paper, which is my preference. Throughout this trial, it was difficult for me to read the jury. In general, when you are lead counsel, it is difficult to read the jury because you are so involved doing things. The feedback we got from Luis and the clients—who were watching more their reactions—was neutral too. We couldn't tell one way or the other, whether we were winning or losing.

We put forth our first witness, Angello. Angello was a manager for the client who had the weaker or smaller case, so to speak. But Angello was very intelligent, articulate, and spoke English at a high level. We also thought that he would be very likeable. For all these reasons, we put him first. Angello testified in detail about the entire seed fiasco. The order, the planting, what came off the ground (or didn't), in a luxury of details. He was thorough and testified from firsthand knowledge. He masterfully fended off massive attacks from both defense lawyers during cross-examination. He had an explanation for every instance where defendants insinuated our processing plants were dirty, the soils were contaminated prior to planting, or you name it, crazy insinuations and inuendo that defense lawyers come up with. He was also not too reactive (like getting mad) and that was good too. We felt he killed it. Overall, we felt really good about our first day at trial. Trial is like a five-set tennis match. You can win the first set but need to still win two more. You can then lose the second set and things are tied. It's the best of five in the end. We had won—we believed—the first set, and that was a good feeling.

Unlike tennis, when you finish the first day of trial around 5:00 p.m., you've got to go to work and prepare for the next day. We went back to the room, to work on strategy and more questionnaires. We decided that the next day we were going to call two employees, one for each company plaintiff. We called a lady who we thought would be a great, knowledgeable witness. We thought we had prepared her well. As it turns out, she was a disaster. Besides the difficulties of the translation, she forgot things, got confused, contradicted herself, and overall did not provide any positive things in terms of proving our case or persuading the jury. Remember that at trial you have to bring evidence (testimony) of all the things in your complaint you need to prove. If you don't, the other side will move for directed verdict and you will not even see a jury. These witnesses did not help us much. Not only was direct bad, but the defense simply destroyed her.

We were depressed. Day two had gone terrible for us. We already knew we had an uphill battle in winning such a difficult case and this did not help. To my surprise, Jorge—who is always upbeat—was feeling down. That completely destroyed me inside. To me, he was the trial expert and if he was down, it was because he felt we were going to lose. I was scared. Luis had the same feeling. We had worked this case for three plus years and a loss would be devastating for the clients, myself, my firm—even financially. We needed to obtain some recovery. But wanting it or not, I was the leader of the whole thing. I had created this case. It was my baby. I had brought it to this point by surviving countless challenges. I couldn't let my emotions bring me down. I did what I always do in these situations: I put on a face like nothing is happening, that everything is OK, even if I don't believe it myself. My first job was to bring Jorge's spirits up. I nudged his shoulder while having a smoke outside the hotel and told him: "Bro, screw them. We are on the right side of history. They sold our clients four-year old rotten seeds. They ruined their businesses. I don't care what happened today. We are not going down without a fight! We are going down swinging!"

My little speech worked a little bit. His spirits improved and he started believing again. We came back to the room to continue working on the next day's testimony.

We decided we were going to call Omar. Omar was a tricky witness. He was the one that was most affected by the whole situation. The business his father had built was almost ruined by the seed fiasco. He even had to sell his house to keep the business afloat. It was very emotional for him, and this made it tricky. He would break in tears during practice as we went through the sequence of events. I was convinced that he was going to break on the stand even more. But I didn't want to play or be casual about this. I did not know how this California jury was going to react to emotions. On the other side, Omar was intelligent, fluent enough in English to skip the interpreter, and had a wealth of knowledge about the situation, especially of damages, where we were weak. As I said earlier, damages are always one of the challenges in business litigation.

We put him on the stand. I had practiced my direct with him forwards and backwards. I thought it was going perfect. When it came to the part where he had to explain what he had to go through to save his company (sell his house) he inevitably got emotional. I believe it came across sincere. He went through all the financial issues including how banks would not lend him operating capital anymore and how his reputation in the industry was ruined. "The rotten seeds guys" they had labeled them. I was truly happy with his testimony. So was my team. We thought we had scored a win. In my mind, we had won the third set.

On the heels of Omar's good testimony, we had to nail it down with our experts. Our main expert, Dr. Coffey, the one who had to convince the jurors with his technical opinion, had a heart attack. Yes, a heart attack. I had been unable to reach him for many hours and I was starting to get worried. It wasn't unusual for him to ghost me, but it was weird that he ghosted me now, during trial. The week prior to trial I had driven and hour and a half to his home with all my files to prep him. Spent three hours going over his testimony and stressed to him the importance that he remains in contact with me at all times. Remember, this is an 83-year-old man. After not getting a hold of him for a while, I get a call from his wife telling me that he had a heart attack and that he was in the hospital. It was deflating. The judge was not going to allow a continuance. We needed his technical input badly. We needed to give the jury the technical reasons; our theory of what caused the infection of the plants and soils.

Our theory hinged heavily on the presence in the seeds of Pythium, a fungus that spreads meteorically in seeds. According to Dr. Coffey, that was the only logical explanation for the disaster our clients experienced. If Pythium was inside the seeds given, then it would have rapidly contaminated the whole thing. There are many species of Pythium, and it is generally found in soils, but it is neutralized by fertilizers and treatment. When it is in the seeds—as some of our lab testing showed—it would have been impossible to neutralize.

As soon as trial ended on Wednesday (our third day), Jorge and I decided to drive to the hospital where Dr. Coffey was. We wanted to know exactly what his medical condition was, so we could report to the judge the next day. In the car, we were down. Jorge and I couldn't believe, that, after all the work we've put, we may lose this case because of this. We also knew that we couldn't push it. We were not going to risk Dr. Coffey's health to win a case.

When we got to the hospital, Dr. Coffey was there lying in bed and in good spirits. Making jokes with the nurses and talking nonstop. Though he was 83, he did not look 83. He also had more energy and brain capacity than any 83-year-old I've ever seen in my life. The nurses were positive about his condition and stated that he may be able to leave the next day in the morning. Dr. Coffey wanted to testify badly. He wanted to go to the courthouse but that did not look like a good option. We offered him that, if he were to testify at all, we'd request to the court that he do it via Zoom. Thankfully, Zoom was already more acceptable in general due to the pandemic.

The next day, as trial begins, and the judge calls for any housekeeping matters, I stand up and say: Yes, Your Honor. The plaintiffs have an issue to address. Our plant pathologist expert had a heart attack yesterday. Everybody in the courtroom was obviously surprised and shocked. I requested the court allow us to call Dr. Coffey not Thursday but Friday and that it be via Zoom. The court was hesitant. The judge did not like the idea of us bringing a witness after we've finished our case-in-chief. The defense, as mean as they were (they had moved to disqualify Dr. Coffey before), was understanding and didn't oppose. In the end, the judge agreed.

Instead of putting Dr. Coffey on the stand, we put forth Mr. Cowheard, our accounting expert. I had high hopes about Cowheard. He was a 50-year-old, intelligent, articulate, knowledgeable, and handsome man. I thought the jury would love him. He went through his damages analysis report forwards and backwards. The damage analysis was very complicated. And Cowheard did a good job at breaking it down for me, so I could better direct examine him. Direct went well but nothing spectacular. Cross-examination was a disaster. He was faced with this nasty California lawyer (did I mention they had 5 different lawyers trying the case?) who was yelling at him and attacking what he insinuated was lack of data and evidence in his opinion. It was mainly a show but to my surprise, Cowheard was flustered. I didn't expect it. He stuttered and did not answer well the questions. Fell into many traps, i.e., questions full of assumptions that he should have unmasked. To my surprise also, the judge—who was strong on civility—allowed the lawyers' show and raising of his voice. Though I thought Cowheard did poorly, I also thought that the lawyer's yelling show and abuse of Cowheard was not going to be well received by the jury, so I was kind of ok with how things went.

The seed manufacturer had his corporate representative present throughout trial. I had listed him as a witness. I had deposed the guy. I knew his testimony would be weak, inconsistent, and good for our case. I didn't call him during my case-in-chief for two reasons. One, the time constrains. I didn't want to use part of our 9 hours of testimony on him. Two, I had asked lead counsel for the seed manufacturer if he was going to call him in his case-in-chief and he unequivocally promised me that he would. We had been asked the same things (who we were going to call) and we had sincerely disclosed who we were going to call, and in what order. At trial, this information is helpful. If you know who is coming next, you can start preparing for cross-examination—be more ready. As it turns out, the attorney cheated and was never going to call his representative. As soon as my case-in-chief was done, the guy left the room. When I asked where he was, he said he had gone back to Washington State. The lawyer blatantly denied to my face that he had promised he was going to call the guy. This was an unforced error: trusting defense counsel. Don't ever trust the opposing lawyer. Be civil, make certain concessions, but do not trust. Don't rely on them doing something that is good for your case. You may run into lying bastards like this one. I brought the issue to the judge. I asked to call him after my case-in-chief. But the judge was not having it. Mr. Ayala, you made a tactical error, you shouldn't have trusted him—were her words, essentially.

The defense did not call any fact witness. All they did was parade their five Ivy league well-paid experts. Experts who really knew nothing about the case, and all they did was pepper the jury with abstract knowledge not based on any test, analysis, or field visit. We thought we did a fantastic job at destroying them on cross. At one point, it was so obvious, that Jorge asked one of them on the stand: "You're just making that up, aren't you?" The jury cracked up in laughter. He said it very naturally, after building up to it. After showing that the guy really had no knowledge about the case and was simply there to impress with his knowledge of pathology, seeds, agricultural logistics, or agricultural economics—depending on the expert. To our surprise though, the jury appeared to have bought into it. That's our impression after the verdict, which I'll tell you about in a bit.

So, it was showtime for Dr. Coffey. He was all smiles on the Zoom screen. Though he hated it, he put on a tie for his testimony. When the clerk was trying to test if he could hear us and called his name, he replied with a loud "hi there" with a strong British accent. It was funny. The jury smiled. Two problems we had with Dr. Coffey. One, he can talk nonstop and go on forever. Two, he could talk in the most sophisticated technical way and is incapable to realize that nobody understands a thing of what he's saying. I had my questions prepared, we had rehearsed them more than once, and I was hopeful. But, as predicted, he went on these long speeches with sophisticated stuff. He somehow managed to be funny though. He's one of these guys that you look at them and laugh. You look at the guy and you are already laughing even before he speaks. I thought that even if the jury did not understand half of what he said, Dr. Coffey still positively impressed them with his wealth of knowledge, and, most importantly, gave them the key idea that Pythium did it.

Before I tell you about Dr. Coffey's cross-examination, let me take a break to tell you something important. We had this super important piece of evidence; a lab analysis of the seeds, on or around the time of the events, from a world-renowned laboratory in Portugal—SGS. The SGS test, which is a sequencing test, showed that the seeds had Pythium in them. The test performed is called NGS, which stands for Next Generation Sequencing. It is a state-of-the-art test that, to put it in lay words, tests the seeds at the molecular level. They chop the hell out of the seed to the molecule level and determine the sequences of DNA or RNA. Based on that, they identify variations of the sequence associated with X or Y disease and then they determine the disease. God knows how they do that. All we understood is that it was reliable, and that it was state-of-the-art. It was a very bad piece of evidence for the defense, whose theory relied on saying that Peruvian water, air, soil, and hands (yes, the hands of the workers) were contaminated. They of course had zero evidence of any of it. The only thing that they could point at were some soil tests from our clients which showed some pathogens common to all soils. Then they would twist that to paint our clients as doing agriculture in dirty soils. But back to the SGS test, one key challenge at trial was going to be getting the SGS report admitted. We had locked down the research on admissibility of third-party reports and the law looked solid. Evidence rulings are wild though. They are decisions made on the spot by a given trial judge and can go either way. You add to that skillful defense counsel who will cry foul up to heaven, and it turns into a difficult proposition. We tried introducing the report first with Omar. Since he had ordered it, we thought of using the business records exception to the hearsay rule. It didn't work. They objected and the judge denied it. We then tried introducing it again during Dr. Coffey's testimony as a report used and reviewed in forming his expert opinion. They objected, and the judge denied it again. Then came cross-examination of their own plant pathologist expert. A very smart guy who unfortunately was on the bad side of the facts. I asked him if he had reviewed the report. I asked him if he knew about SGS, the company. I asked if NGS was a reliable method of testing. He testified that SGS was one of the best in the business, that NGS was reliable, and he had no reason to question the results of the report. Right after that, I moved again. They objected, but the judge allowed it.

It was a big win. The jury was going to see in the jury room the report showing that the seeds had Pythium in them. Along with that, they were going to hear Dr. Coffey say Pythium *ad nauseam.* I was feeling good.

Back to Dr. Coffey's cross. Cross was, to put it simple, hilarious. Dr. Coffey destroyed opposing counsel. He simply couldn't believe how dumb he was (from his genius perspective) and couldn't help being hyper sarcastic. I honestly don't recall many of the details of his responses, but the jury was cracking up more than once. He was very good also at making the point that our clients had been given rotten seeds (the seeds were 4 years old at the time they arrived to our client's fields), that seeds are live organisms with an immune system, and that their life span is 3 years on average. That 4-year-old seeds were dead on arrival! It's hard to recreate it in writing, but the way he said these things was hilarious. We had plenty of scientific articles backing the idea that pea seeds' life span is 3 years on average. But the defense produced this one article—which should not have been admitted into evidence, in my opinion—that said seeds could live up to 20 years. Dr. Coffey could not help but laugh at that and said something to the tune of "there's a crazy person in every field, even in the scientific community." Though he was rough in expressing this idea, he was right in substance. The article was an outlier. Overall, when you add and subtract, I thought Dr. Coffey's testimony was very positive for us. The jury never knew, of course, that he had just had a heart attack. The defense had explicitly requested that none of that was even hinted at. We agreed, and specifically warned Dr. Coffey against insinuating anything related to his health.

The seed seller called the owner, a lawyer and veteran. The guy put on a drama about what a hard worker he was, how he had served in the military, and how poor he was now. He had a sore throat and raspy voice and exacerbated it intentionally on the stand. The jury, unfortunately, bought into his story. No sugarcoating, this guy was a jerk. He knew exactly was he was doing, and he did it well. He should have checked he was selling us dead seeds and didn't. End of story. All his veteran background and health issues should not have been mentioned. They got away with it despite our objections. We also didn't want to attack a "veteran" too much. I may be biased but I deposed this guy. He's a prick. There's nothing to be sorry about this guy. He put on a show.

It was clear on Friday that we were not going to be done by Friday. The judge had already told us we would finish on Monday. On Friday, though, we would close all the evidence. Right after the close of the evidence, the seed manufacturer moved for directed verdict. The main argument was—you guessed it—the economic loss rule. (Remember, we had to overcome the economic loss rule in order to seek damages beyond the purchase price of the seeds. If the economic loss rule applied, we couldn't seek damages for lost profits, contamination to other fields, loss of business goodwill, etc.). We were surprised. Our research showed that, absent privity (i.e., a contract relationship), the economic loss rule did not apply; and we didn't have a contract with the manufacturer. There were even cases from the Central District (our court) that supported us. But there were also some conflicting opinions from the Northern District, the court right north of ours. The research clearly showed that was a minority view and, given the cases from the Central District (from our judge's colleagues, essentially), we thought there was no shot. How wrong I was. The judge—literally—believed her colleagues were wrong. Mr. Ayala, she told me, I understand the cases you are citing, what I am telling you is that I disagree with my colleagues. These opinions are not binding on me. What were the chances? I was deflated. One of the issues connected to this—don't ask me the logic now—was that, if the judge allowed us to seek damages beyond those directly connected to these particular seeds, we had to itemize or split the damage calculation. If it was impossible to split, then she was not going to allow us to seek damages for non-pea-seed related loss. If we were able, then she was going to allow the jury to decide whether to award us damages for (1) the loss directly related to the pea seeds, and/or (2) loss beyond the seeds themselves.

I am not sure if you get the picture, but I was standing by my chair, speaking off the cuff, pushing my brain to its limits, while sleep deprived, arguing against a lawyer from the five-lawyer defense team, whose sole task at trial was this moment. That was her single job. I, with limited preparation, misguided, confident in what the research showed, and a heavy accent, was arguing in open court, in one of the most important federal district courts in the country, that our case should survive. It was literally that, survival. The damages connected to the pea seeds would have been insignificant. It would have virtually meant a loss. In the end, the judge was going to allow us to present evidence that our damages were itemizable. She said I had to do an "offer of proof." I had no idea what that meant. That's not a term we use here in Florida. I just understood the "proof" part of it. I had to bring in "proof," I thought. But I didn't know how. We had no witnesses left. My only shot—I thought—was to get it in through their witnesses. I tried to do so in the cross of one of their damage experts. In one of the breaks, I called our damage expert and told him to try to do a breakdown of damages: the ones connected to the pea seeds, and the ones connected to the rest. He was awesome. He understood my stress and worked hard, and in an hour or so, he had a calculation that he sent to my email and explained to me on the phone. His calculation (and the logic) seemed reasonable, and it still gave us something around half a million in damages for the pea-seed related damage. I tried to get that exhibit admitted in cross, asking questions to the defense damage expert witness. They objected the heck out of it. I didn't know what to do. I felt I was trying to do what the judge had just asked me: to bring in the "offer of proof" thing. I didn't know what to do to overcome the defense's objection, so I called a sidebar.[20]

It was literally the most stressful sidebar of my life. It was me and four other lawyers—who were very tall by the way—facing the judge on her also very tall podium. I felt like an ant. I said, Judge, you asked me for proof, I am trying to get this itemization prepared by our accountant expert which I shared beforehand with defense counsel to show that our damages are itemizable. They objected the hell out of it, with 100 arguments, one of which being that the itemization was vague and not reliable. The judge said: Mr. Ayala, oh, that's your offer of proof? I said, yes, yes, Your Honor, offer of proof! After further back and forth, the judge said she was going to allow it into evidence. She thought that if it was prepared by an expert who had been on the stand, was shared with the defense, and there was no indication otherwise that it was unreliable, she would allow it, and she invited the defense to submit their own rebuttal of Mr. Cowheard's itemization of damages. The whole sidebar was around 15 minutes. I was so drained after that. The idea that our case could be virtually tossed there, without even getting to the jury because of the economic loss rule and this damages thing was so stressful. But, hey, we had dodged a bullet. The jury was going to decide our case, on the full spectrum of it, and potentially award all the categories of damages we were seeking. (For lawyers, the offer of

---

[20] Sidebars are meetings right next to the judge so the jury can't hear what we are talking about.

proof thing is similar to our idea of proffer, which is essentially, evidence provided by the lawyer).

I still get stressed as I recall these events. This, I am telling you, is literally the essence of what I do. It's stressful. It's dealing with the unknown. It's dealing with powerful talented adversaries. It's being underfunded. But it's doing it all—and going through it all—because of the passion for the game. It's always been to me not about the money but about the glory.

It is so important to me to pursue causes that I believe in, and fight, fight hard. I truly believed in this case, and I was going to fight until the end. If I lost, I'd still be at peace because I gave it my all. You know deep inside—always—when you've given it your all or close to all. There will be mistakes that you'll see in retrospect. Hindsight is always 20/20. But you'll know in your heart that the effort was there. That effort, in my opinion, makes you a better human.

* * *

We were all done and then came closing statements time. At that point, we really did not have a good idea as to what the jury was going to decide. Our perception—which we didn't trust—was that the jury was going to give us something. We thought it was going to be very hard, based on what we and they had presented, that the jury was going to be: "Yeah, the seeds were alright, you don't know how to plant." That was not going to happen. The question was, is the jury going to award us significant damages? For us, winning started at seven figures or anything close to seven figures. Even 900K would have been subjectively counted as a win for us. The client's number was a little higher, but they don't really understand how the system works, evidence, the rules of trial, or the damages allowed under the law, which are always less than the client's actual damages.

The uncertainty made me prepare for closing statements even more. I've never prepared a speech so much. I barely slept. I googled everything there is to know about closing statements. I typed my statement word for word, and then memorized it. I don't believe in reading speeches. I practiced it many times in front of the mirror in my hotel room. I ran it by Jorge. I thought it covered all the things it needed to cover. I went through all the pieces of evidence which supported our case to remind the jury of what they had seen. I prepared a nice PowerPoint presentation so they could follow. It was around 17 minutes long. Delivery wasn't so good. I was not satisfied. I thought I got nervous, spoke too fast, and did not connect well with the jury. Compared to opposing counsel, a lady, one of the partners at the firm, it was a slam dunk. She was really a disaster. That, at least, made me feel better.

It was the end; our fate was now in the jury's hands. This almost 4-year journey, and most recently 4-week journey in California, was about to be over. Whatever happened, I hugged Jorge, and I told him with confidence: Bro, we left it all in the field, no regrets whatever happens. Still, deliberation time is always anxiety time. Even if the decision comes after one hour, it feels like an eternity. It wasn't too long in this case. It only took a few hours (three or four) until the jury came out with a verdict. We walked back to the courtroom and sat down to hear the verdict. We wouldn't have a copy of it until later, so we had to make sure we understood exactly what we were getting at that time. Remember, there are multiple defendants and multiple causes of action as to each. The jury had a bit of a complicated verdict form.

The first heartbreak was that the jury let the seed seller go scot-free. We were destroyed when that part was read. We couldn't believe they let the crooked guy walk. Then came the judgment against the seed manufacturer. The jury awarded around 260K to one of our clients, and about 60K to the other. The jury also awarded the seed manufacturer some setoff for "contributory negligence." All in all, the total verdict was worth shy of 300K. (We had settlement offers higher than that). It was a verdict for the plaintiffs, but effectively, a loss. The clients were sad. We were sad, but thought that we had given it our all, and at least we got something. "It could have been worse," we thought. For good or for bad, we were also relieved that it was over. It's just such a stressful, restless time. At least, we would get to go back home, and turn the page; move on with our lives. And so would the clients. They wanted their day in court, and they had it. We made it happen, and we gave them, considering the circumstances, resources, the best shot they were going to have in a foreign court with two essentially local defendants.

It was a hell of a case. One of the most important in my career—even if it didn't turn out the way we wanted. I've had a bigger verdict in a less consequential case. But this one is, for sure, the most important one. The number of things I learned are hard to count. But most importantly, this is what I do. I am in the middle of stressful situations all the time. As a trial lawyer, as a businessman, as a crisis manager. I wouldn't have it any other way though. If it's not me, who is going to do it? Who is going to represent these clients nobody wants? Do I just go back and do personal injury and receive policy limit checks pre-trial? There are good fights there too. But who wants to take on this unlikely, hard to win, laborious, consumer cases? Few. I want to be one of those few. I am not nearly as well off (from my practice) as similar attorneys; attorneys that are my age and do trial work or run their practices. My financial success has come from very good business moves and deals I've made outside the practice and from opportunities that have come to me by "owning a practice." Having a firm, even if broke, opens up business opportunities, access to capital with banks, and other important connections. I am thankful that I have been able to make smart moves business-wise, and now I am in a privileged financial position.

I don't care about money though. Not one bit. As I write this now, I don't even own a car; I ride a bike. When it comes to the law, once I fell in love with it, it's never been about the money for me, it's all 100% of it about the glory. I don't feel I've achieved it, but when and if I do, I'll seek more. Like Roberto Gómez Bolaños (aka Chespirito) once said, you are never old if you have projects. Seek projects.

CONCLUSION

There's no secret formula to build a law firm. Law firm types and practices are as varied as there are colors. Start small, keep the basics and fundamentals strong, build a brand over time. Define the environment where you want to practice. I had it clear in my mind, from the very beginning, that my law firm will not be a place of "nastiness." In my law firm, nobody will ever yell at someone. I wanted a peaceful environment where to practice the profession I love. I hope this book, has given you two things regarding building your practice:

1. At least one idea about what to do.
2. At least a little bit of motivation to go and do it.

ACKNOWLEDGEMENTS

Thank you to everybody that in one way or another help this book become a reality. First, to my editor and now partner Luis Quesada, Esq. One of the most talented writers I've ever seen. A man whose brain naturally breeds rock-solid logical arguments. The firm is so lucky to have you. Thank you for all you do. Thank you for having my back, always.

To Farai, our wonderful marketing manager who I assigned the project of publishing this book and dealing with all the logistics involved in it. She did not hesitate for one second. She researched what had to be done, found the right professionals, and got it done. Farai, thank you so much for making it happen.

To my team, because, inevitably, in the past year or so, I've taken hours of my time that should have been dedicated to the firm's cases to write this book. In that process, they've taken a bigger burden, and had my back. Special mention to Ryan, who has now become a key part of the firm, and its expansion plan. Thanks a million Ryan. We are so lucky you are part of this.

Special mention also to Sulay Garcia too. Financial manager, office manager, senior litigation paralegal, immigration paralegal, HR, you name it. The number of hats you wear at this little business is hard to count. The firm is so lucky to have you too. Your loyalty and commitment, through seven years now, do not go unnoticed to me; not a single day.

To Juan Carlos Gomez, who hates the spotlight, but whom I had to dedicate an entire chapter of this book because, really, without him, this firm would not exist. Juan Carlos, if heaven exists, you have a VIP table there, I am sure.

To Eric, Igor, Jorge, and Oscar for their kind forewords to this book. You guys are gold. Your friendship is gold. Lucky call you friends, colleagues, or business partners. I can't wait to continue to see all our firms thrive in the future.

To all of you who follow my journey. Thank you for your support. It means a lot.